From Playpen To Podium

OTHER WORKS BY JEFFREY L. MYERS

For Such a Time as This: Becoming a Millennial Leader
(Nashville, TN: Lifeway, 1999).

*Secrets of the World-Changers: How to Achieve Lasting Influence
as a Leader* (Dayton, TN: Heartland Educational
Consultants, 1998).

*Of Knights and Fair Maidens: A Radical New Way to Develop
Old-Fashioned Relationships* (Dayton, TN: Heartland
Educational Consultants, 1996).

From Playpen To Podium

Noble Publishing Associates
1311 N.E.134th Street, Suite 2A
Vancouver, WA 98685
www.noblepublishing.com
800-225-5259

From Playpen to Podium
©1997 by Jeffrey L. Myers
Published by Noble Publishing Associates
1311 N.E. 134th Street, Suite 2A
Vancouver, WA 98685
Ph:800-225-5259

ISBN 1-56857-068-6

Printed in China

00 01 02 03 04 05 06 / 10 9 8 7 6 5 4 3 2

DEDICATION

It requires patience and dedication to transform a self-conscious, shy and bumbling young person into a confident communicator. Jerry McCollough, H. Gene Specht, Louise Brokaw and David Boman all poured themselves into my life, and I am forever grateful. In addition, I have benefited from the ideas and encouragement of my mother and father ever since they talked me into taking a speech class in 9th grade. May all of their efforts bear fruit in the next generation of leaders!

TABLE OF CONTENTS

CHAPTER ONE

YOUR CHILD: AN OUTSTANDING COMMUNICATOR

The cardboard box full of small slips of paper moved slowly up and down the aisles of gleaming desks. On each slip of paper was a number, one through twenty-seven, which would determine the order of each student's demise; it was oral book report day. A very fair method, to be sure, was this teacher's way of determining the order in which each student would present. Trembling fingers reached into the box to pull out slips of paper. There were many sighs of relief as the box passed from one student to the next.

You can teach your child to communicate effectively!

One extremely shy young man was struck with horror. Not only had he forgotten that this was the day to begin oral book reports, he had forgotten to read his chosen book! Heart pounding, he reached into the box, hoping for a number which would allow him until the next day to prepare. Shaking hands unfolded the small paper scrap. *Number...* one. Terrified and embarrassed, he announced that he was unprepared, put his head on his desk, and wept.

Several years later, another young man of the same age walked confidently into a room full of stern-looking adults. He faced his audience squarely and delivered a five-minute oration with a clear, convincing voice, earnest gestures and a compelling story. When all twenty participants had given their speeches, the results were tallied. The young man was awarded first prize!

This book will

help your

child become

the kind of

purposeful,

personable,

prudent,

polite and

persuasive

person he

was created

to be.

I happen to know the difference between the two young men. The second young man began communication training at a much earlier age, at home, with the help of his parents. Although his parents possessed no formal speech training, they taught instinctively, using hints gained from years of helping their oldest child develop communication skills.

How do I know? Because the second young man was my brother, Tim. The first child? That was me.

After my awful experience, our parents made "communication building" a priority. They encouraged me to take a speech class, got me signed up for the high school debate team, volunteered their weekends to judge debates, drove vans of noisy high school students to speech tournaments, and became involved in communication activities themselves. The example, inspiration, advice, and persistence of my parents, speech teachers and debate coaches opened the door to my becoming a high school state debate champion and later a nationally ranked collegiate debater, as well as student government president of a university of 7,000 students.

Since that first experience, by the grace of God, I have delivered well over 2,000 speeches to audiences ranging from graduate classes to keynote addresses to thousands of professional people, as well as innumerable radio and television interviews. Learning to communicate well has allowed me to walk through doors that I might not even have *knocked* on otherwise.

One reason I'm excited about this book is that it contains the wonderful counsel and advice that changed my life so dramatically.

Another reason I am so enthusiastic about the material in this book is this simple, incredible premise: *everything my teachers did for me, you can do for your child, and you can do it even more effectively.* Your home can be a living, breathing communication workshop far better than any class your child will ever take. Moreover, there is no need to wait until your child is of high school age. Everything you need to know is right here, and you can start your child at birth.

Perhaps a disclaimer is in order here. Despite first appearances, the purpose of this book is not to turn young children into wondrous and charming public speakers, though I believe that skill will emerge in your child if you follow the strategies described here. The real purpose of this book is to help you provide a strong foundation for your child so that he will become an outstanding communicator in *every* area of life, throughout life, whether that is in one-on-one relationships or in front of huge audiences.

Just as I must disclaim something, I must also claim something. As a follower of Jesus Christ, I strive to base all of the principles in this book on God's Word, the Holy Bible (by the way, I *am* a fallible human being, so please don't take everything I say as gospel!). I say this so that fellow believers will understand the perspective from which I am writing: I believe God wants His people to lead by example, and this book will help your child become the kind of purposeful, personable, prudent, polite and persuasive person he was created to be. In short, this book will help your child develop *practical* leadership skills which glorify God.

When a craftsman sets his mind on accomplishing a large task, he first makes sure he has the necessary tools. This book contains all of the tools you need for the task of giving your child the communication advantage in every area of life. You will discover how to help your child

Your home can be a living, breathing communication workshop far better than any class your child will ever take.

become more comfortable in social situations, think more clearly, read and write more effectively, take a stand more boldly, analyze more carefully, and speak more articulately.

Here is what this book will do for you:

- Demonstrate how "communication building" fits into the goals that you have for your child.

- Show you the "six pillars" of communication success, and give you clear ideas on how to build them into the structure of your home.

- Give you dozens of easy-to-use ideas to build specific kinds of communication skills from infancy through the teen years.

- Demonstrate the most important things to know in preparing and giving a speech and how to make use of them.

This book is designed to help you pursue excellence, not perfection, for your child. You *can* help your child improve his ability to communicate so he can be what God wants him to be. And what better motivation can parents have than to see their children grow to be successful in the things that matter most? Proverbs 23:24-25 says, "The father of the righteous will greatly rejoice, and he who begets a wise child will delight in him. Let your father and your mother be glad, and let her who bore you rejoice." I pray this will come true for you and your family in a whole new way because of this book.

By the way, what *are* those things which matter most to parents? In the next chapter, I will discuss the goals which you as a parent probably have for your child and how communication skills will help you reach those goals.

CHAPTER TWO

HOW COMMUNICATION SKILLS RELATE TO YOUR GOALS FOR YOUR CHILD

THE COMMUNICATION ADVANTAGE

In a complex and competitive world, children who possess excellent communication skills will have a tremendous advantage over those who do not. Most jobs, even so-called "unskilled" positions, require public speaking, and even companies hiring for jobs which focus primarily on technical skills are increasingly hiring those who possess strong communication abilities over those who do not. Currently, seven out of ten jobs require good speech skills.

Moreover, those who communicate their thoughts and ideas clearly and fluently are often chosen to be leaders. The great speakers in our nation's history, William Jennings Bryan, Patrick Henry, Abraham Lincoln, Martin Luther King, Jr. and hundreds of others, all recognized the creative power of words to reach deep into the hearts of their audiences.

Listed here are some of the goals parents have for their children which may be better reached through the communication skills emphasized in this book.

Those who communicate their thoughts and ideas clearly and fluently are often chosen to be leaders.

GOALS MOST PARENTS HAVE FOR
THEIR CHILDREN

"I want my child to have a sense of purpose in life." It has been said that the number one fear of youth today is that they will not discover their purpose in life. Hopelessness and boredom reign supreme among young people who live for the moment, having been convinced that life is really a big mistake and that existence is meaningless. Such is the natural consequence of a philosophy of life without God. The Christian life can and should be dramatically different. Jesus said, "I have come that they might have life, and have it to the full" (John 10:10, NIV). Moreover, Colossians 3:23 says that whatever we do, we are to do it "heartily," which literally translates "with all the life that is in us (NIV)."

Purpose emerges, in part, through action; we find our sense of purpose through *trying out* lots of things. A young person who knows how to communicate well with others and is willing to speak publicly will discover a whole new world of opportunities. I have seen young people develop communication skills and then start Bible studies, plan outreach crusades, testify before state legislatures, appear on television talk shows, conduct radio interviews, participate in press conferences, speak to community groups, and run political campaigns. Through such activities, your child will catch a vision for the world around him, and ultimately for the things of God. This book will give you dozens of ideas for how to use communication building to help your child discover a sense of purpose in life.

"I want my child to be aware of the world around him." Awareness is a foundational principle of good communication skills, and good communication skills lead to greater awareness. Unfortunately, many young people are unaware of the world around them and unconcerned that there is a world outside of themselves.

In his letter to the Philippians, the Apostle Paul calls us to do nothing out of selfish ambition, but to put the needs of others before ourselves (Philippians 2:3-4). As we learn to communicate more effectively, we become more sensitive to those around us, and more aware of significance of everyday events. Communication skills are closely tied to intelligence: not a higher I. Q., but "practical intelligence" or "common sense." Excellent communication skills will help your child use his five senses to become *aware* of the world around him. This book will give you creative ways to help your child in this area.

We learn primarily by reading, which allows us to absorb new information, and writing, which allows us **"I want my child to be a better learner."** to translate those thoughts into a meaningful new form. Poor oral communication skills are a significant reason for young people failing in reading and writing.

Conversely, learning to communicate well strengthens reading and writing skills. One study noted that students who display the greatest mastery of words exhibit a higher level of scholastic ability than their counterparts regardless of the area of study. Other studies simply show that children who are given the opportunity to communicate orally, and are encouraged to use language as a tool to satisfy their curiosity, develop a stronger foundation of language learning which ultimately makes the learning of reading and writing more profound. This book will show you how your child's improving communication skills will strengthen his reading and writing skills.

Communicating well helps children *think* more effectively, because there is a living connection between **"I want my child to be a creative thinker."** thoughts and words. Speech helps us create the structures in our mind that promote creativity and a quick wit. A whole host of academic studies have proven that confident communicators are those who can "think on their feet," that is, quickly and accurately understand a situation and formulate a response to it. This book will share some powerful secrets to boosting your child's ability to think well.

"I want my child to be poised." People expect good communicators to know how to act in a socially appropriate manner. If our behavior is awkward and embarrassing, or if we are not sure of how to communicate our thoughts clearly, we are seen as unintelligent by our teachers and bosses. On the other hand, polished communication skills open doors throughout life. Zig Ziglar quotes a series of studies in his book *Top Performance* which claim that 85 percent of the reason one gets a job, keeps a job, and moves ahead in that job has to do with *people skills and people knowledge!* Through training in communication skills, your child will become a more graceful and pleasant person. This book highlights some creative ideas that can make poise happen.

"I want my child to relate well to others." Dr. Frank Dance, an expert on speech development, believes that one of the main purposes of communication is to link us to our environment. Communication brings your child in contact with others, and allows him to listen and share with others. Children who "link-up" to their environment well find it easier to relate to others, and therefore enjoy smoother social interaction. Your child will attract others, because attraction is more a function of how well we relate to others and express concern for them than how physically beautiful we are. This vital skill is called empathy. This book will help you create a strong foundation for empathetic communication by focusing on the skills of listening and conversation.

REACHING YOUR GOALS THROUGH COMMUNICATION TRAINING

Quite simply, the goals that parents have for their children are *integrally related* to communication skills. Armed with good communication skills, young people gain the confidence they need to take a stand for what is right, when everyone else is retreating. Communication training shows young people how to make contributions, exert influence, and create positive peer pressure, setting a good example that other children may be willing to follow. Using this book, you will be able to add a rich new dimension to your child training, imparting the skills that your child needs to survive and mature into a thoughtful, intelligent, caring and successful person.

Each of the significant communication skills we just discussed are pillars which, based on the foundation of a strong home environment, support the "roof" of communication excellence, no matter the age of your child. The next chapter will describe the foundation and the pillars to help you decide on a strategy for communication excellence.

CHAPTER THREE

THE SIX PILLARS OF COMMUNICATION EXCELLENCE

THE SPIRITUAL MANTLE OF FAMILY COMMUNICATION

Henrietta Mears was perhaps one of the most gifted communicators of the twentieth century. Founder of the Sunday School movement as we know it, her influence on the Christian leaders of today was nothing short of profound. During the course of her life, she founded several ministries, including Gospel Light Publications and the Forest Home Conference Center. Among the hundreds of people she discipled were Billy Graham, Bill Bright of Campus Crusade International, and Richard Halverson, the late chaplain of the U. S. Senate.

Few individuals could serve as a better model of a confident communicator. Barbara Hudson Powers, in *The Henrietta Mears Story,* makes clear the key to Miss Mears' success:

> One thrilling thing…about the life of Henrietta Mears is the great spiritual heritage she has received. The scope of her life has been tremendous; even more tremendous is the spiritual influence of her forebears, which can be traced back through at least five generations, and the spiritual 'mantle' that has been handed down on the maternal side from one generation to the next. Truly this is a witness to the scriptural promise "that it may go well with thee, and with thy children after thee."

Family communication in the home is the number one issue in the scholarly study of leadership.

Miss Mears' spiritual legacy was strong in large measure because her spiritual heritage was strong. The same is true in every area of life; every strong building rests on a solid foundation. According to Frank Pace, an expert on why people become leaders, family communication in the home is the number one issue in the scholarly study of leadership. If your family encourages communication and provides opportunities for reasoned discussion and influence, your child's influence on the world around him is almost certain to be greater.

BUILDING A STRUCTURE FOR COMMUNICATION EXCELLENCE

Imagine it this way; the foundation of communication excellence, and indeed of your child's impact on the world, is a home environment conducive to developing strong communication skills. If this foundation is strong, then one can confidently place on it pillars strong enough to support the roof. If we put a strong foundation in place, and create a pillar to represent each of the six "goals that parents have for their children" as discussed in chapter two, the roof of communication excellence is well supported. It will be strong, stable and protective of the very elements that lend it support.

Just so we can better visualize the process, here is how the structure might look:

This first section of this book addresses the foundation and each of the six pillars, one chapter for each. It will show you, with dozens of practical, helpful ideas, how to enhance your child's communication skills in a way that builds a strong foundation for life-long communication excellence. Look for exciting, usable games and projects to help your child improve communicatively, no matter what his age. You can start with infants, teenagers or anywhere in between. It's that simple.

HOW TO PUT THE SIX PILLARS TO WORK IN YOUR HOME

Here's how you can use this book: If you are looking for general improvement in your child's communication skills, read the first eight chapters, begin putting some of the ideas into practice, and then gradually begin trying out some of the projects geared toward the specific age of your child. If you desire to help your child "brush up" on a particular skill, look for the "stamps" which accompany each project, indicating which of the pillars addresses that skill most directly. Here are the stamps which you will find throughout these chapters, along with a brief description of each.

Home Environment

Home Environment results from parents teaching and modeling communication skills in everything they do, often unconsciously, as a way of life. It supports the pillars of communication excellence in the same way that warm clothes, healthy food, and a clean, pleasant house support the health and happiness of your child.

Purpose

Purpose results from a child's recognition of his parents' love, as well as a sense of the excitement and meaning of everyday life. It supports communication excellence by taking away fear and making your child's communication appealing to others. In turn, communication excellence generates enthusiasm for other areas of your child's life.

Awareness

Awareness results from a child's curiosity about the world, and it supports communication excellence by giving your child the ability to become more aware of the experiences of others, how to reach the heart of an audience, and how to effectively translate his own experiences into meaningful information for an audience.

Learning

Learning results from a child's love of gaining new information, and it supports communication excellence by giving your child a base of experience from which to speak. In turn, communication excellence generates a heightened sense of the importance of words, making a deeper level of expression possible.

Creative Thinking

Creative Thinking results from experiences which allow your child to be creative and to think in interesting, exciting ways. It supports communication excellence by giving your child a unique, exciting perspective on life, spurring him on to a new level of quick, powerful thinking.

Poise

Poise results from a child learning to be comfortable in a wide variety of settings. It raises your child's comfort level and skill in front of an audience or in any social situation in which he might find himself.

Empathy

Empathy results from a child being trained to listen to and learn from the experiences of others. It improves your child's skill in relating to others, increasing his attractiveness to them and thus the power of his message.

READY, SET, GROW!

This book is both a course of study and a reference tool. Use it however it works best for you, but *use it!* The impact on the life of your child will be profound *and* far-reaching.

CHAPTER FOUR

ADJUSTING YOUR HOME ENVIRONMENT TO FOCUS ON COMMUNICATION EXCELLENCE

COMMUNICATION EXCELLENCE BEGINS AT HOME

The home environment is the foundation on which communication success rests. People who believe that a classroom is the best environment for learning will consider this a radically unorthodox idea. However, child researcher Dr. Mabel Rice demonstrated that since communication skills are *natural* to a child, simply being in an environment where communication takes place is stimulation enough for a child to learn to communicate. There are certain foundations which even the best classroom teacher cannot create for you, and this is one of them. As far as communication skills are concerned, you are the best teacher your child will ever have.

Since communication skills develop and mature naturally in the home, any activity which creates a more stimulating home environment should result in better communication skills. Thus, the focus of this chapter is to suggest ideas which will help you create a home environment

As far as communication skills are concerned, you are the best teacher your child will ever have.

that fosters a dramatic improvement in your child's willing-ness and ability to communicate.

HOW TO CREATE AN "OVER THE T.O.P." HOME ENVIRONMENT

Three areas in which you can begin improving your home's communication environment include using your *time* wisely, creating an environment of *openness* to com-munication, and being *persistent* in the example you set through your own communication. These three areas form a memorable acrostic:

T = TIME
Use the time you have with your child wisely.

O = OPENNESS
Foster openness so that your family wants to com-municate.

P = PERSISTENCE
Persist in setting a good example of communica-tion.

Let's take a few minutes and review each briefly.

T = TIME

How can your family, busy as it is, find time to foster better communication skills? Here are some ideas that fit into the schedule of things you already do:

1. **Eat meals together.** Dorthea McCarthy discovered that children who score highest on language tests usu-ally come from families who have breakfast and sup-per together. Meal time is probably the best time for two-way conversation and family bonding. Try it out!

If you have a difficult time stimulating conversation, here are three simple ways to get things going:

- Bring something to share. Ask each family member to bring something to discuss, whether it is what happened at work, what was learned in math class, how the favored team fared in the "big game," or a question about a political candidate.

- Bring questions. Ask each family member to come to the table with a question they can ask another family member. This reinforces listening skills and stimulates general interest in other family members.

- Start a sharing sack. Ruth Beechick suggests that each person place a note in the sack before dinner. The note can be a Bible verse, joke, passage from a book, news article, cartoon, answer to prayer, etc. When conversation lulls, draw something out of the sack and let the contributor talk for awhile.

2. **Use car time wisely.** How much car time does your family spend with each person off in his own little world? Here are some ways you can utilize car time to stimulate communication:

- Listen to story tapes or a radio talk show and discuss it.

- Review what is expected of your child in an upcoming situation.

- Ask your newly reading child to call out words he knows on passing signs.

- Play a game in which you call out a word and the next person must think of a word which begins with the last letter of yours, and so on.

An easy way to

gain more time

together as a

family is to

limit television

viewing.

The average

American

watches

television 28

hours a week,

time that could

almost certainly

be better

invested.

- Speculate imaginatively about the place you are visiting. Make up stories about fictional characters who might have been there many years ago.

- Purchase pre-made car games, or modify games such as *Twenty Questions*.

- Play the alphabet game: compete to find the letters of the alphabet, in order, on passing road signs or billboards.

- Make up stories. One person starts the story, and each person adds a paragraph.

- Design a small song book with your family's favorite songs.

3. **Develop a family night each week.** Each family member can have the opportunity to decide what you should do during that time. Consider doing something outside the home once each month. The other nights, have fun at home and save money!

- Go see a play.

- Rent a movie and discuss it.

- Read aloud together.

- Visit friends.

- Have a game night.

- Play "Kick the Can" or a family sport.

Using activities like these, you will significantly increase the number of hours in each week when you can turn your attention toward communication skills. Yet there is one other suggestion, controversial as it may be. An easy way to gain more time together as a family is to limit television viewing. The average American watches television 28 hours a week, time that could almost certainly be better invested. At the same time, don't feel pressured to use every single minute productively. Just add a few simple activities here and there, and you will start getting results.

In order to make your family time together more productive, you will want to create an environment in which each member of the family feels comfortable communicating with the rest of the family. This aspect of the environment is called openness.

O = OPENNESS

In *Six* Weeks *to Better Parenting*, Caryl Waller Krueger says that surveys of parents have revealed five areas where parents would like to improve relations with their children: finding the time and topics to discuss with their children, expressing patience and understanding, having time to enjoy children in a recreational way, following through on discipline, and giving children responsibilities that will help them grow. Amazingly, many of these desires may be reached through activities that also build communication skills. Here are some simple things you can do to open up the communication environment of your home and spend more time with your child in ways that make a difference:

1. **Create experiences through language.** Strive to put your thoughts and the experiences you have together with your child into words. For example, when driving over a railroad bridge, say things like, "We're going over a railroad track. What travels on the railroad track? Why do we have railroad tracks?" Talk about trains, discuss what they carry and share a story about the railroad or "the little train that could."

Openness in

your home is

sometimes hard

to develop.

It may feel

awkward. Your

child may be

suspicious.

But stick

with it!

2. **Affirm your love for your child.** Communicate the certainty of your love and acceptance of him. Do it even when you must communicate displeasure. Children have very short memories; they will easily interpret irritation or silence as a *withdrawal* of love.

3. **Organize family devotions.** Use family time to lead your children to a better understanding of God's Word. Occasionally ask an older child to read the devotional material (an excellent book is *Leading Little Ones to God,* published by Baker Bookhouse). Give that child the right to ask questions of other family members about the reading. He will not only reflect more carefully as he reads, he will also make sure the others are listening! When you read the devotional material, ask a question or two of the family before you begin and have them listen for the answer.

4. **Host family meetings.** Family meetings give your child a forum in which his input matters. It also encourages him to think through his comments, basing them on reasonable evidence, and taking the perspective of others. It can be an excellent time to read a book together, teach your child how to take a stand for his faith, discuss heroes, share vacation plans, address current events, make plans together, and work through problems. Some parents opt to present problems to the family and ask for possible solutions. However, those parents should check with each other before turning a problem over to the family to solve, and they should never burden their child with problems he cannot help solve (such as, "Where are we going to get money to buy food this month?"). Once concluded, the whole family must abide by the decision of the group, or your child will quickly begin to think of family decision-making as a waste of time.

Openness to communication in your home is sometimes hard to develop. It may feel awkward. Your child may be suspicious, but stick with it! Perhaps the most significant way to show that you're serious about openness to communication is to consider our next topic, how to be persistent in improving your own communication skills.

P = PERSISTENCE

Parents are the most significant models for how children should act. Studies in behavior demonstrate that children will more frequently do as the parents do, rather than what the parents say, if the two are inconsistent. This is especially true in communication. As the *Becoming a Nation of Readers* report noted, "Language frames the world the child knows; the richer the language, the richer the child's world. Especially with a small child, it is better to say too much than too little." If you are not a talkative person, then concentrate on at least communicating more than commands and admonishments. Your persistence will reap meaningful benefits in the life of your child. Here are some ideas to consider:

1. **Express positive emotions.** Your child takes cues from you regarding how expressive he should be, so use a wide vocal range and let your voice convey what you feel, especially with positive emotions such as happiness, excitement, suspense, and joy. Point out to your child that certain situations demand certain tones of voice, and that vocal variety is useful for communicating in "real life."

2. **Send consistent messages.** A parent who maintains a smiling face while using an angry voice will confuse his child. The most clear message results when all aspects of your communication are giving the same message, so match your tone with your gestures, eye contact, and facial expressions.

Studies in behavior demonstrate that children will more frequently do as the parents do, rather that what the parents say, if the two are inconsistent.

3. **Make eye contact positive.** Eye contact is an extremely powerful means of communicating positively, yet it is often used in a negative way (as in, *"Look at me when I am talking to you!"*). Children who are asked for eye contact only when being reprimanded will view it as unpleasant. Instead, connect eye contact with a smile and pleasant words.

4. **Express your feelings carefully.** When you feel angry about your child's behavior, do not say, *"You make me so angry."* This rids you of responsibility for your own feelings, and indicates that the problem is a permanent part of the child. Try instead to describe his behavior to him by saying, *"I feel very frustrated when you behave that way."* This indicates to the child that you are *not* frustrated at who he is, but at his behavior *at that moment.* In addition, carefully control your voice during discipline. A parent who responds in a loud, irritable voice to even the most minor infraction will find himself not taken seriously in the event of a major infraction. Ask yourself: "Are my emotions in check?" Children will learn emotional control by your example.

5. **Be sensitive to the level of your child.** Don't assume that your child always understands what is said to him, or that he means what he says. The way children learn language varies: sometimes they understand words that they do not use, sometimes they form rough definitions of words based on the context in which they are used, and sometimes they simply parrot words they've heard. Often the best way you can help is to be patient with them!

6. **Communicate clearly.** Have you ever been frustrated when your child doesn't understand and act on what you say? Sometimes it is pure mischief. However, if there are a number of distractions in the environment, your communication will be unclear, somewhat

like trying to talk through a cheap set of walkie-talkies. The way to overcome noise is by saying the same thing in several different ways to ensure that your meaning is understood. The "70/30 Rule" was designed by George A. Miller, an expert on humans' capacity to process information. He concluded that the best way to make ourselves understood is to spend 30% of our time stating in simple terms what we want the other person to understand, and 70% giving examples and painting brief pictures of the outcomes we desire. This is true with parent-child communication as well. By making yourself clear, and asking your child to repeat back to you what you want him to do, you will minimize misunderstandings.

HOW TO BECOME MORE AWARE OF THE COMMUNICATION ENVIRONMENT IN YOUR HOME

Perhaps the best way to improve the communication environment of your home is to take a "self-test" each day. Ask yourself questions like, "Are my voice and facial expressions consistent?", "How can I set a better example of expressiveness for my children?", "When was the last time I used eye contact to communicate in a positive way with my child?", "Does my communication reduce uncertainty about my love and acceptance of my child?", "Do I communicate unconditional love even when I must punish my child?", "When was the last time I really *showed* my child that I love him?", "How can I use words to create new experiences for my child?", "What one thing can I do to make my child's language environment richer today?" "Have I communicated more than just short verbalizations with my child today?", or the ultimate, "If communication were a measure of wealth, would we be rich or poor today?"

These questions are important because they turn your attention to the home environment as the foundation of

Model and teach your children to communicate more effectively, and the pillars which are built on this foundation will stand strong and true.

communication excellence. Such a foundation is not built overnight, and it must be repaired frequently. The strength of the home environment is a meaningful, subtle and vital part of our relationship with the rest of the world. Model and teach your children to communicate more effectively, and the pillars which are built on this foundation will stand strong and true.

It is now time to move on to a discussion of the first pillar, purpose in life. Purpose, as we shall see, is not really a communication skill. However, a child who is developing a strong sense of purpose will be primed and ready to quickly learn whatever skills are necessary.

CHAPTER FIVE

HELPING STRENGTHEN YOUR CHILD'S SENSE OF PURPOSE IN LIFE

SENSE OF PURPOSE AS A FOUNDATION FOR COMMUNICATION DEVELOPMENT

The first pillar that must be built on the foundation provided by the home environment is *purpose*. Purpose is the source of and motivation for all skills, especially communication skills. Great communication comes from the heart, not the head. Once when teaching a university speech class, I had a student who struggled terribly in the class; he was shy, unwilling to communicate expressively, and disorganized. One day he gave a speech warning of the dangers of alcoholism that caught me completely off guard. He violated virtually every aspect of the assignment, yet gave a truly tremendous presentation. I stood back and let him go; he had something that no instructor could teach in just one semester.

Later, I tried to pinpoint what had changed. It was as if the student had a *passion* for his subject; he really *believed* what he was saying. He saw significance in it. Based on whatever tragic life events compelled him to

Great communication comes from the heart, not the head.

give the presentation, he had *lived* the significance in it. Then it dawned on me; his speech was so infused with meaning that it was as if it was part of his very purpose for existence.

Then I understood. It *did* contain his purpose for existence. That is why it was truly great.

After thinking it through, I scrapped my old lecture on "overcoming fear" in public speaking, and replaced it with a new approach based on "purpose in life." If an individual can understand his purpose in life, and use that purpose to energize what he does, then whether it is in a speech or just in daily communication, he will advance far beyond what would otherwise have been thought possible.

There are many historical examples of a sense of purpose igniting the desire to communicate an important message to the world. William Wilberforce gave hundreds of speeches before Parliament, most of them urging his colleagues to abolish the immoral practice of slavery. He was a hated man. Wilberforce's speeches became so unpopular that members of parliament would file out of the chamber when he rose to speak. Ultimately, however, his burning passion for justice resulted in the abolition of the British slave trade.

Wilberforce's success was fueled not by his desire to put himself in front of lots of people, but by a holy passion and a love for those who could not help themselves. His epitaph in the Westminster Abbey bears witness to this fact, noting that he was "among the foremost to fix the character of his times."

Purpose in life cannot really be considered a communication skill, but it is so integral to communication that we dare not leave it alone. It is purpose in life which makes it easy to get up in the morning, to plan carefully the impact we wish to have on the world around us, and to stand courageously in spite of great difficulty. Purpose makes timid people strong, propelling them beyond the ordinary into a kind of greatness that few understand. D. L. Moody embodied this kind of purpose. He said, "The world has yet to see what will happen when a man will truly get on fire for God. By God's grace, I intend to be that man." Moody impacted the lives of tens and perhaps hundreds of thousands, and his legacy is still doing so today.

This chapter will give some rudimentary ideas about how to assist your child in developing a sense of purpose in life. If the lives of students with whom I've worked are any indication, the result will be a much stronger platform on which to build communication skills. The three points which I consider most important in developing purpose in life are these: live as if your child has a purpose, help your child develop a sense of significance, and be a cheerleader for your child.

LIVE AS IF YOUR CHILD HAS A PURPOSE

Scripture is quite clear that human beings are endowed with purpose by their Creator. The psalmist writes:

"For you created my inmost being;
  you knit me together in my mother's womb.
I praise you because I am fearfully and wonderfully made;
  your works are wonderful, I know that full well.
My frame was not hidden from you when I was made
  in the secret place.
When I was woven together in the depths of the earth,
  your eyes saw my unformed body.
All the days ordained for me were written in your
  book before one of them came to be."
                                        Psalm 139:13-16 (NIV)

It is purpose in life which makes it easy to get up in the morning, to plan carefully the impact we wish to have on the world around us, and to stand courageously in spite of great difficulty.

Purpose in

life means

enthusiasm

based on the

realization

that our

lives have

meaning and

that every

event in

them is

infused with

significance.

Purpose in life means *enthusiasm* based on the realization that our lives have meaning and that every event in them is infused with significance. We thus see the world in a meaningful way and recognize our importance in it.

I believe that above all else, to treat children *as if they have purpose* is the most significant way to help them develop a sense of purpose in life. Here are some questions you can use to help decipher that sense of purpose for your child:

1. **Questions to discover the significance of past events and present condition.**

   - Why do you suppose God chose to have you born when he did?

   - Why do you suppose God gave you the family that he did?

   - Why do you suppose God allowed you to grow up where he did?

   - Why do you suppose God allowed certain things to happen to you?

2. **Questions to discover the interests and abilities God has given you.**

   - Who are three people who have made an impression on your life? How did God work through them?

   - What sorts of things have you accomplished which gave you a tremendous sense of satisfaction?

   - What one thing would you share with an audience if you only had one speech left in life?

- When you think about the future of the nation, what is one area in which you can make a difference?

3. Questions to help you discern your ministry.

- What particular burdens for the ministry do you have?

- What special opportunities and needs are put before you?

- What do you feel called, compelled and obligated to do?

- What do you enjoy doing for the Lord?

- What talents and skills has God given you that can be dedicated to the Lord and his service?

- Who can you ask that might be able to help you discern answers to those questions?

4. Questions you can use with your child every day.

- What was the best thing that happened to you today?

- What happened during your day that was funny?

- What would you do differently if you had it to do over again?

- What was the strangest thing that happened to you today?

Questions that allow you to reflect on the meaning and significance of life are a significant step toward purpose in life. They give you a framework for interpreting what happens, no matter how mundane.

One caution: be careful not to give your child the impression that his answer is set in concrete and may never change. Questions such as these form a *benchmark* which helps us see more clearly how God works in our lives. Our understanding of our purpose emerges and becomes clearer as we grow older, so be patient!

HELPING YOUR CHILD DEVELOP A SENSE OF PURPOSE

Often it is difficult for parents to keep the lines of communication open with their children. Whether through the stress and strain of everyday life, or simply being preoccupied, we unintentionally put our children on hold. Here are some powerful tips on imparting a sense of significance which take just a few moments but which your child will always remember:

- Tell him frequently that you love him and that you are glad he is in your family.

- Give him an idea of his "place" in the family by highlighting for him and other family members the role he plays, i.e., "No one else in our family would have noticed that. Think what we would have missed! I'm so glad you're part of our family!"

- Show him baby pictures and convey the sense of excitement you had while waiting to have him, as well as your thrill of holding him in your arms.

- Tell him stories about your family: the different places you have lived, things that happened to you or your relatives, and how you met your mate.

- Use "I can" language that demonstrates that you have responsibility for your life, that it is not out of your control. For instance, replace "I can't" with "I choose not to," "I'll try" with "I will" or "I won't," and "You make me so mad" with "I feel very angry when you do that." Encourage your child to make these changes as well.

• Let your child see you in action making a difference in the life of another person in your community or in a significant cause.

• Say, "I may not always like what you do or approve of it, but no matter what, I will never stop loving you."

• Focus on positive emotions: "Isn't it great to..."

• Make sure your child knows that the time you spend together is meaningful: "I would rather be spending this time with you than doing anything else in the world."

• Express interest in what is important to him: "I don't know very much about this, but I am interested in learning about what *you* are interested in!"

Simple adjustments such as these can have a profound, lasting impact in the life of your child.

HELPING YOUR CHILD MAINTAIN A SENSE OF PURPOSE

The final role of parents in imparting a sense of purpose is that of cheerleader. A coach motivates his players to top performance by providing opportunities to practice winning strategies and then serving as cheerleader, applauding the team's success and helping its members work through the pain of failure.

Here are some ways you can be a cheerleader for your child:

- Reinforce your child's confidence in himself and give him opportunities to decide things on his own. Caryl Waller Krueger suggests that this may be as simple as appreciating his decisions: "You did the right thing to not open the door to that stranger" or "How wise of you to turn off the oven so the meat loaf wouldn't burn."

- Refrain from "managing" his communication. Dr. James Dobson says that children feel most confident when they believe their parents have confidence and trust in them. Do you become tense and nervous when your child speaks to others? Do you interrupt to explain what he was *really* trying to say, or do you let him speak for himself, even if he doesn't say it quite the way you would have wished?

- Reward your child for noticeable performance. When I was growing up, my parents rewarded my brother and me with a shiny quarter every time someone complimented *them* on *our* good behavior.

- Spend meaningful sharing time with your child. Find a time each day to visit. Share with him a letter you received from a missionary friend, or have him read it aloud to you. Help your child focus on the positive experiences of the day. Take him with you when you run errands, and use this time to listen to your child and find out more about his thoughts and interests.

- Focus your time and energy on positive people and characteristics. Your child should know that it is okay to admire the positive characteristics that another person possesses. In many of the summer camps at which I teach, we ask questions such as, "Who is one person you admire and why?" Sometimes I design questions to stimulate students' thinking such as, "If you had to go into hiding for being a Christian, who would you want to have with you to take care of you?" or, "If you could be Tonto, who would you have as your Lone Ranger?" Understanding the heroic is important to our own character development.

SENSE OF PURPOSE: A SOURCE OF ENERGY

Your child's confidence level will increase as he sees the purpose in everyday events, and senses from you that his life has meaning and significance. He may feel more free to embrace hobbies or causes with gusto, having experiences that will be vital for future communication confidence.

The next step in building communication skills is to help your child become more aware of the world around. Awareness ties your child together with others and allows him to learn the lessons which are so vital to outstanding communication skill.

CHAPTER SIX

HELPING YOUR CHILD BECOME MORE AWARE OF THE WORLD AROUND HIM

THE IMPORTANCE OF AWARENESS IN COMMUNICATION DEVELOPMENT

"I just started looking around," said my brother Tim. "I looked at billboards and thought, 'How *negative* they all seem to be. Companies using women in bikinis to sell beer, cigarettes and whiskey. I have got to get our community focused on *positive* media images.'" Tim didn't just look; he took action by starting a small billboard company, Positive Media, to create and place billboards with a positive message. Tim raised thousands of dollars to put up billboards. How did he, at age sixteen, raise the money? "I just observed people who had money, and I asked them for it," he explains, matter-of-factly. In starting Positive Media, Tim took action based on an awareness which escaped most adults, and ultimately developed a vision which significantly impacted his community.

Observation: seeing what is going on around you. Awareness: knowing what it means. It's not just a gift for police detectives! Every child can benefit from becoming

Great communicators cultivate an awareness of their surroundings.

Great

communicators

harness the

powers of

physical

eyesight to

develop

spiritual

insight.

aware of the world around. This chapter highlights aware-ness as a vital pillar in the building of communication. Here are some of the distinguishing marks of people who possess a greater awareness than those around them:

- They see more clearly into the needs and aspirations of others. They are more attuned to "unspoken" com-munication.

- They discern untruths more quickly.

- They sense possibilities which go unnoticed by others.

- They enjoy life more, because their senses are height-ened.

- They can quickly figure out solutions to difficult prob-lems.

- They drink deeply from the well of lessons that nature and other people have to teach.

- They develop a stronger sense about how others might be persuaded to change what they believe and do.

Great communicators cultivate an awareness of their surroundings. Everyday occurrences take on greater mean-ing; they harness the powers of *physical eyesight* to develop *spiritual insight*. The human condition and the search for meaning become eminently more understandable. Aware-ness helps writers be brilliant, speakers witty, and coun-selors adept at assessing the needs of clients.

In addition to being the source of great communication skill, awareness is a foundational principle of the Christian faith. The twenty-fourth proverb of Solomon, verses 11-12 says:

"Rescue those being led away to death; hold back those staggering toward slaughter. If you say, 'But we knew nothing about this,' does not he who weighs the heart perceive it? Will he not repay each person according to what he has done?" (NIV)

The implication is that we are to observe the world around us, and to act on what we observe to the glory of God and the benefit of others. Other passages of Scripture give the same message: "Where there is no vision, the people perish." Jesus said, in Matthew 15:14, "If the blind lead the blind, both will fall into the ditch." Being sensitive to the world around us often involves asking "What would Jesus do?" when we confront difficult issues.

Being aware of the world around him, your child can better understand its problems, relish its joys, and utilize its potential. Your child can rise above society's expectations and be truly set apart for a special purpose.

Two physical senses play into awareness: hearing and seeing. These senses become gateways to the mind. The key to raising awareness is intensifying your child's ability to get information and process it. What follows are some activities which will help you help your child in this regard.

HELPING YOUR CHILD BECOME MORE OBSERVANT

You can help your child become more aware of the world around him through simple activities that focus on observation skills. Here are some activities that will work easily into your busy schedule.

- Develop special observation times. I occasionally take a child with me on errands, stopping for a soft drink on the way home. As we sit in the restaurant, we observe other people. I ask questions like, "What do you suppose that woman is like? Friendly? Unfriendly? Why do you think that?" or, "Why do you suppose that man looks happy? What might have happened that would put him in a good mood?" We also observe negative behaviors. "Why does that boy look down at the floor most of the time? What would make him want to do that? How can we make sure we don't act like that?" As you listen and respond, your child will develop a whole new repertoire of observation skills.

- Start a "Sense Journal." Ask your child for one observation each day that you can record in a journal for him. I often write my own observations on note cards, so I can file them for later use in speech or book illustrations. In fact, I encourage the college and seminary students that I teach to do the same thing. Lavish praise on your child for thorough, creative observations.

- Play "What can you see?" games. For a younger child, test his skills of observation through questions about things in his immediate environment. Ask questions like, "Which three items in this room are orange?" "Which of these three drinking glasses can hold more water?" Questions should emphasize three factors: perception (questions which ask, "Which is bigger, smaller, wider, longer, rougher, brighter," etc.), understanding (questions which ask, "Why, how, when, where, who"), and value (questions which ask, "Which of these do you prefer and why?").

- Involve the child in your activity. If you are looking at a magazine, show him some pictures and ask questions about them. If you are baking, ask your child to help make measurements.

- Play the "Block game." With one set of blocks, create a structure. Have your child observe the structure for a few seconds, then go in another room and recreate the structure with an identical set of blocks. Praise your child for accuracy and quickness in his reconstruction. Better yet, take turns, and allow him to test *your* observation skills.

- Play the "Selling game." Choose a household item and ask your child to develop a "sales pitch," pointing out the item's good qualities. This game is often funny, sometimes silly, but always creative!

- Encourage choice-making. Choices heighten the need for awareness. They require children to discern right from wrong and to distinguish between good and great, better and best. Caryl Waller Krueger suggests giving children as many choices as possible:

  "Of these three vegetables, which one do you want for dinner?"
  "Would you like to watch television program A or program B?"
  "Would you like to stay up late tonight or tomorrow night?"

Regardless of the choices made, be sure to enforce the consequences of the decision. Do not let your child talk you into allowing him to stay up late both nights! TIP: Limit the choices you offer to a very young child who may not understand that "choice" means one or the other, and may be baffled and upset as a result.

- Take a trust walk. In a trust walk, you blindfold your child and lead him around, giving him opportunities to touch, smell, listen and taste. Removing one of the senses, sight, will cause him to rely more on the others.

Developing an

awareness of

the world will

provide the

source of

information for

speeches, it will

help your child

understand

others more

clearly, and it

will deepen

the well of

resources from

which he can

draw as an

outstanding

communicator.

After about ten minutes, remove the blindfold and ask your child to identify what happened.

Observation games should be a source of challenge and fun. If you get to the point where you are "drilling" your child, or he loses interest, stop for a while. Gradually you will notice your child developing observation skills on his own.

INTERPRETING WHAT YOU OBSERVE

Interpreting involves forming an image of the source's trustworthiness and competence, and detecting the message's emotional impact. Depending on the age of the child, use children's stories, magazine advertisements, pictures, television programs and news stories to demonstrate how to interpret the messages we receive.

Here are some ways to discuss interpretation:

- Discuss believability. Define and discuss what it means to trust. What makes a person trustworthy? How can *we* be more trustworthy? What evidence is there that a particular message is trustworthy? Is it good evidence?

- Consider the persuasive appeal. What is this particular story or advertisement or program trying to get you to feel or do?

- Discuss the motives to which the message is appealing. To what are the advertisers appealing in order to get you to buy their product? Do they claim that their product will make you more attractive, more outgoing, or more wealthy? Can they really deliver what they say? If not, how does that affect their trustworthiness?

Here are three print advertisements which are similar to those found in the classified section of many newspapers and magazines. Find some in your newspaper and discuss them with your child.

- WATCH FAT WASTE AWAY! New cream designed by a team of doctors and nutritionists will shrink unwanted fat cells and leave you with a beautiful body. No exercise or special diet needed. Just wait until your friends notice!

- FREE HAWAIIAN VACATION! Just come in and test drive any of this year's models, and receive a vacation for two in Hawaii. Round trip airfare for one and four nights' accommodations included. When you're dreamin' away in tropical paradise, you'll be glad you came in!

- GOVERNMENT SURPLUS AUCTION! Cars for $50, jeeps for $25. Boats, yachts, equipment; all dirt cheap! Send $25 plus $5 shipping/handling for catalog.

Interpreting a message is the first step in understanding it. The second step is to evaluate it. Evaluating information allows your child to develop impressions about the things he sees and make sense of them for his own life.

EVALUATING WHAT YOU OBSERVE

Evaluating means testing ideas for truth or falsehood and deciding how much of a message to accept or reject. You can enhance your child's ability to evaluate messages by presenting "what if" scenarios geared to the age of the child. Here are some examples:

- "What should you do?" activities. Tell the story of a child who lies to his parents, or read "The Boy Who Cried Wolf." Your child can evaluate what the child in the story should and should not have done and why. Other scenarios could include:

What if...

— a stranger asked you if you wanted a ride?

— someone told you that God does not exist?

— you were a guest at someone's house and you spilled your drink?

• Evaluate advertising messages. Examine advertisements in the mail, in newspaper, and magazines and on television. Help your child discern, for example, the truth in an automobile advertisement. What does it mean to lease a car for $199 a month? What other costs might be hidden? When you see a television report about a news story which you know is slanted, quiz your child about what sort of questions he might ask the reporter. Consider questions such as, "How do you know that is true?" and "Where do you get your information?"

• Observe the folly of the wicked. In Proverbs 24:30-34, the author tells of observing and learning lessons from the mistakes of a lazy man: "I went past the field of the sluggard, past the vineyard of the man who lacks judgement; thorns had come up everywhere, the ground was covered with weeds, and the stone wall was in ruins. I *applied my heart* to what I *observed* and *learned a lesson* from what I *saw*" (NIV) (Italics mine). We learn much of our practical morality from observing how acting foolishly leads to horrible consequences. If you see a picture of someone who is being led away to prison, or if you see a drunkard on the street, discuss with your child how that person might have gotten himself into that situation. The ability to observe and then *avoid* actions with negative consequences is of lifetime benefit.

Developing an awareness of the world around is a skill with lifelong benefit to your child. It will provide the source of information for speeches, it will help him understand others more clearly, and it will deepen the well of resources from which he can draw as an outstanding communicator.

This "deep well of resources" will make learning an adventure. The next chapter will show how communication skills and a love of learning are tied together, serving as another strong pillar in our building of communication.

CHAPTER SEVEN

HOW YOUR CHILD CAN BECOME A BETTER LEARNER

HOW LEARNING AND COMMUNICATION SKILLS ARE RELATED

Three-and-a-half-year-old Rebekah crawled into my lap with a second grade storybook. "May I read to you?" she inquired sweetly. Having never refused such a generous offer, I said, "You bet!" I awaited the typical "reading" of children that age, namely, an oral interpretation of the pictures. To my amazement, the book contained few pictures. I thought, "Boy, this must be a really dull book!" Much to my amazement, Rebekah slowly read, and I mean *read*, the story to me.

Without a doubt, Rebekah was an unusual little girl. There is something unique about her family which helps me understand her early advancement and obvious joy for reading. She lives in a family with parents who love to learn. Her parents communicate their love for learning in such a way that Rebekah naturally wants to learn more. In conversation around the dinner table they weave fantastic tales, share the exciting plot from the book they've been

The foundation you build in your home for learning will provide a strong support for your child's developing communication skills.

"The limits of

my language

mean the limits

of my world."

—Wittgenstein

reading, and create suspense about a story they will read as a family that night.

The third pillar of the building of communication is *learning*. The ability to learn, as well as the love of learning, provides lifelong tools for developing wisdom and knowledge. The foundation you build in your home for learning will provide a strong support for your child's developing communication skills, which will, in turn, give him further opportunities to learn. In this chapter we will discuss some easy-to-implement ideas to make your child *want* to learn! Let's begin by examining the connection between learning and communication skills.

We noted earlier that children who are given the opportunity to communicate orally, and are encouraged to use language as a tool to satisfy their curiosity, develop a stronger foundation of language learning which ultimately makes learning more profound. The philosopher Ludwig Wittgenstein explained it this way, "The limits of my language mean the limits of my world." Those with powerful communication skills will be granted access to the storehouse of knowledge that is the foundation of our civilization. Without that access, our civilization will not long be civilized, since citizens who cannot learn from the past cannot avoid its mistakes or plan thoughtfully for the future.

This chapter will present four ways you can create enthusiasm for learning in your home: reading, modeling enthusiasm for learning, making learning fun, and learning together.

THE READING ROAD
TO COMMUNCIATION EXCELLENCE

"The single most important activity for building the knowledge required for eventual success in reading is reading aloud to children," states the 1985 report of the

Commission on Reading. Top authorities in the study of reading skills appear to be in universal agreement on this point. Because reading is the means by which one acquires in-depth knowledge throughout a lifetime, it will never be a waste of time to emphasize reading in your home. This process begins when the child is very young and continues even after the child learns to read to himself. Reading together provides a vital bond between parent and child.

According to Mary Jo Puckett-Cliat and Jean M. Shaw, reading aloud to your child helps him understand how language is put together, forming the foundation for his own language use. He will learn thinking skills and develop an intuitive understanding of logical thinking and cause-and-effect relationships. This ultimately leads him to deep, rich "imagining" skills. The mind and imagination of children crave stimulation, and reading aloud or telling stories fulfills this need, motivating them to a life-long love of reading.

Here are some ways to inject your home with enthusiasm for reading:

1. **Start reading early.** Experts suggest that parents begin reading to children as young as a month or two old! Studies by child education experts show a direct and long-term benefit, demonstrating that if you can start the process early, the empty framework of your child's mind will fill up much more quickly.

2. **Read enthusiastically.** When reading to your child, play the role of each character, adding vocal inflection and actions to bring the characters to life.

3. **Read with suspense.** Create a sense of suspense and wonder through reading. If you are reading a book that will take more than one day, for example, don't stop reading at the end of the chapter. Stop at a

The mind and imagination of children crave stimulation, and reading aloud or telling stories fulfills this need, motivating them to a life-long love of reading.

highly suspenseful moment in the story. Both of you will have something to look forward to the next day!

4. **Read inquisitively.** Have characters in the book "ask questions" of the child, or have the child ask questions of the characters, to which you make up appropriate responses. While reading *Jack and the Beanstalk*, for example, say, "I have a question for Jack. 'Jack, what did you think when you saw how tall the beanstalk had grown?'"

5. **Make reading adventurous.** You can add a fun twist to reading and help your child grow in imagination by approaching reading in a larger context. If your child reads a book about another part of the world, help bring it to life by asking him to find that place on the map, draw pictures about various scenes, list questions to ask someone who has been there, or look up additional information in the encyclopedia.

6. **Use poetry.** Many adults have had bad experiences with poetry, but poetry reinforces the natural rhythm of life. King David filled his thoughts and worship with poetic songs and essays, reflecting on the nature of God and the world around him. In some inexplicable way, singing songs and reciting poems which have a strong meter actually help the mind become organized. This is especially true for young children. Second, poetry teaches intense language skills. It trains children to convey complex thoughts using few words. Find poetry books for children at a used bookstore. Encourage your child to memorize a poem or two if he is so inclined, or even write poetry of his own.

7. **Overcome the vocabulary barrier.** Be certain your child understands the vocabulary and ideas presented in the reading. Asking questions or making comments

about the reading lowers your child's level of frustration and creates additional interest.

Reading aloud is valuable for its own sake. It has the additional advantage of encouraging excellent oral communication skills. If you have time for nothing else, be sure to make time for reading!

The next step in creating enthusiasm for learning is to actually model *enthusiasm* for learning. Consider the eye-opening suggestions in this next section.

HOW TO MODEL ENTHUSIASM FOR LEARNING

Modeling good communication skills to your child will give him a significant boost toward becoming a curious, inquisitive learner. Consider this statement from Professors Kimmel and Segal:

> Several studies of children from widely varied backgrounds who learned to read early and remained good readers throughout their school years revealed that they had something in common. They all had been read to regularly from early childhood and had as models adults or older children who read for pleasure.

Some time ago I spent time with a family whose son had just turned two. Because of his mother's inquisitiveness about the world around them, he developed an enormous vocabulary for his age. I discovered this while taking a walk with him. "Look, Jacob, there is a flower," I commented as we passed a garden. He stopped, studied the particular flower I was pointing to and said, "Not flower, *rose!*" I stood corrected, and quite amazed. The child continues to be far ahead of his class not because his parents are more brilliant than other parents, but because they model good learning.

Children who

are good

readers come

from families

where parents

enjoy reading.

"Enforced

illiteracy,"

knowing how

to read but

not doing so,

is the second

greatest

educational

problem

facing our

nation, next

to not being

able to read

at all.

Here are some helpful ways to model learning in your home:

1. **Devote family time to learning.** Laura Ingalls Wilder told tales of earlier times, when fathers read to the family while the girls served or mended and the boys whittled or worked with leather. Give this old-fashioned idea a try. Sometimes you can read aloud to the whole family, other times you can make it a silent reading time when parents read the newspaper or magazine and children read their own books.

2. **Reinforce learning through activity.** Make home-made books for your young child, with pictures of family members, your house, car, dog, toys, and other recognizable items. As you read them, point out the real object so the connection between the picture and the real object becomes clear.

3. **Talk about learning.** Talk with your older child about the books he is reading. For a younger child, reinforce the words he knows or letters he recognizes. You can conduct this activity by watching signs while riding in the car.

4. **Focus on the interesting parts of learning.** While it will later be important for your child to understand why stories work the way they do, it is best to listen carefully, asking specific questions, but allowing your child to tell his version from start to finish. Moreover, avoid questions about vocabulary, sentence structure, plot, or anything that will diminish his enthusiasm for the excitement wrapped up in the story itself. As Ruth Beechick notes, focusing on such details is like an artist saying, "Don't get carried away, folks; it's really only oils and colors and brush strokes." Beechick suggests that you talk instead about the construction of the story and

how the characters manifested positive or negative character traits ("How did they demonstrate honesty, diligence, courage, kindness, or obedience?"). Your child can even project himself into the story and speculate about how he would act in a given situation.

It has been said that "enforced illiteracy," knowing how to read but not doing so, is the second greatest educational problem facing our nation, next to not being able to read at all. On the other hand, few things are more exciting than a family which models learning. The results are so *obvious*. Your child will not only stand out among his peers, he will have a strong foundation for the things that matter most in life.

How to Make Learning Fun

Children do not gain the ability to think abstractly until they are about thirteen years of age. Before that, their thinking is very concrete, craving practical application. Knowing this, you can structure activities to accompany learning which build enthusiasm and enhance your child's ability to retain key points. Here are some creative ideas, each of which is expanded in the projects section of this book:

1. **Reinforce the alphabet.** Sing through the alphabet, or stick some magnetic letters to the refrigerator. Your child can learn the letters and form words, even devising games to entertain himself while you are fixing dinner. Toy stores also sell foam letters which stick to bathtub tiles when wet, so you can turn bath time into learning time.

2. **Use art.** Allow your child to paint, mold, draw or construct scenes from a book he has read using the various art techniques at your disposal. These can be collected

In the long

run, children

prefer toys

which allow

them to

create things.

in a book or posted on the wall. *Any activity which enhances your child's imagination and ability to relate what he knows to reality will reinforce communication skills.*

3. **Create advertisements.** Ruth Beechick also suggests that you permit your child to develop written and oral advertisements about the book he is reading, with the goal of persuading someone else to read it. This is a fun way for the child to synthesize the main points of the book, deduce what makes the book suspenseful, and expand his imagination.

4. **Dictate stories and journals.** If your child is of pre-school age, he can "write" stories by dictating them to you. These stories may describe a vacation, an exciting day, or imaginative situations which you make up together. Illustrate the book with drawings, photographs, magazine pictures, or a greeting card. On really special occasions, you can have the book laminated and bound at a local photocopy store. These books will be treasured and re-read many times.

5. **Have the child read aloud to you.** The primary purpose of this activity is not to critique your child's reading level, but to have an opportunity to show how proud you are of his skills. There is absolutely nothing like a parent's encouragement to inspire a child to continue reading!

When buying toys for your child, remember that in the long run, children prefer toys which allow them to create things. These kinds of toys last longer and yield more benefits than battery powered cars or robots.

The final key to enthusiastic learning in the home is to learn *together* as a family. Since traveling as a family is a perfect opportunity for learning as a family, we will focus our attention on this point in the next section.

Learning Together Through Travel

Traveling together as a family is often stressful, and many a parent has felt severe disappointment when the child does not seem as interested in a historical sight or nature exhibit as the parent does. Yet in spite of the downside, traveling is one of the most powerful ways to create enthusiasm for learning. Studies demonstrate that children who have had travel experiences have a larger vocabulary and better communication ability than those who have not.

Here are two ideas for making more of this potential learning time:

1. **Create enthusiasm for travel in advance.** Experiences are always more meaningful if your child is prepared for what he will see. Whether you plan to attend a play, visit a Civil War battlefield, or take in a major league baseball game, brief the child in advance. For a play, set up the plot in a way he will understand. For a battlefield, describe why it was important, borrow some mementoes from a friend, read stories about the battle or ones similar to it, and rent a film. For a game, give your child some idea of what to expect and be sure he possesses a rudimentary understanding of how the game is played. I knew of one college-age girl whose father had never explained the game of baseball to her. She grew up believing that a "strike" occurred when the batter flinched as the ball crossed the plate! Needless to say, she did not enjoy baseball.

2. **Make the most of travel.** Collect brochures in advance and set realistic expectations. Give your child his own set of maps so he can chart the family's progress (laminate them if possible), and ask him to help plan stops and decide which sights to see. You might even appoint an older child "tour guide" to "lead" small parts of the

Children who have had travel experiences have a larger vocabulary and better communication ability than those who have not.

trip. This will encourage him to observe much more than he might otherwise notice.

In conclusion, a love of learning and communication skills fit hand in hand. If your child comes to love learning, developing advanced communication skills will be no problem whatsoever. The result will be a child who is confident, knowledgeable, and more prepared to take on the challenges of life.

The ability to learn and the love of learning are enhanced by the techniques of creative thinking, the next pillar in the building of communication.

CHAPTER EIGHT

HELP YOUR CHILD BECOME A MORE CREATIVE THINKER

THE NATURE OF THOUGHT

Contrary to popular belief, great thinkers are not necessarily like *Star Trek's* "Spock," thinking in a logical, computer-like fashion. Instead, the key to highly effective thinking is the ability to *think outside of the boundaries* which bind everyone else. Consider the following:

- Thomas Edison and physicist Richard Feynman both attributed their intellectual prowess to their ability to think in analogies, or creative word pictures, that simplified outrageously complex ideas.

- Albert Einstein, according to nearly all accounts, was extremely creative, almost childlike in his fascination with the creativity of nature. His creativity freed him from the strictures of thought which had bound physicists for centuries.

- A shockingly high number of computer programmers, mathematicians, engineers and physicists are also

Those who learn to communicate well stand a better chance of learning to think more clearly and creatively than those who do not.

To the degree

that we are

made in the

image of

God, we can

think, speak

and create in

wonderfully

complex and

beautiful ways.

highly accomplished musicians and artists, dispelling the myth that creativity and logical thought are somehow two separate phenomena. One of the computer programming companies in a city where I used to live encourages lunch-time classical music sessions. I'm told that these programmers are some of the most talented musicians in town.

L. S. Vygorsky, a Russian researcher, believed that the speech structures mastered by the child become the basic structures of thinking. In other words, those who learn to communicate well stand a better chance of learning to think more clearly and creatively than those who do not. In focusing on creative thinking, this chapter promotes the idea that as your child learns to communicate more effectively, he will become more *creative*, and that creativity is the key to higher order thinking.

THE NATURE OF CREATIVITY

Thinking, creativity, and communication skills reflect the nature of God. The Gospel of John says, "In the beginning was the *Word*," or "*logos*," which in Greek means both *word* and *mind*. God *created* the universe in his *mind*, and then through the *Word* (personified in Jesus Christ) he *spoke* it into existence. To the degree that we are made in the image of God, we can think, speak and create in wonderfully complex and beautiful ways.

It seems perfectly natural, based on the above, to work on enhancing thinking skills through practicing communication skills. The best way to enhance creative thinking is through acts of creativity that employ thinking and communication skills in a unique, powerful way. Two practical ways of utilizing the creative principle are drama and story-telling.

DRAMA:
LETTING THE IMAGINATION COMMUNICATE

Drama is a natural way to get children to communicate in a fun, yet non-threatening manner. Caryl Waller Krueger explains that drama teaches skills of intelligence, conviction, clarity, imagination and creativity. While we will focus more intensely on drama in the practical application section of this book, it may be helpful to outline several different ways drama can be used to reinforce communication skills and allow children to work together to accomplish a goal.

1. **Act out reading.** Your child can *be* the "little engine that could" or David swinging the slingshot at Goliath. Acting out reading is a natural way to transfer "book" knowledge into actual experience.

2. **View professionally produced plays.** A play often costs less than a movie, provided it is performed by a community theater group or local high school or college. There is nothing like live theater to spark a child's interest in drama.

3. **Perform spontaneous plays.** Mrs. Krueger suggests that you set the scene by giving a few sentences of introduction, then having the child carry out the play without structure or script. This enhances his ability to think on his feet and develop plot structure creatively and intuitively.

4. **Enact plays about real world experiences.** Use a play to act out things such as attending a new church, going on an airplane, attending a party, or visiting someone your child doesn't know. In fact, drama can be used to reinforce visiting and conversation skills.

5. **Play charades.** Choose a character for each child to act out until the others in the room can guess what it is. This helps children learn to use their bodies in a dramatic way. It also shows them how to use their nervous energy to *boost* their performance rather than paralyze them.

6. **Host a neighborhood play.** Allow your child to gather neighborhood children for a production. Volunteer your backyard or garage, prepare snacks, and invite the other parents to watch. You will be amazed at the embellishment which children add to the set, comic relief, and fake fights!

7. **Present puppet shows.** Old socks, knickknacks such as sponges and yarn, and even paper sacks make great puppets. Give your child an old sheet or newspapers which he can paint or color for set design.

8. **Create Bible pantomimes.** Together you and your child can devise pantomimes of Scripture passages. Consider the possibilities of passages such as Proverbs 23:19-21, "Listen, my son, and be wise, and keep your heart on the right path. Do not join those who drink too much wine or gorge themselves on meat, for drunkards and gluttons become poor, and drowsiness clothes them in rags." (NIV) Your family will find new meaning in Scripture as you guess the story being acted out. Your child will *feel* the meaning as he or she acts out Moses' amazement at the parting of the Red Sea, Mary's gratefulness as she anointed Jesus' feet and wiped them with her hair, and Naaman's expression when the little slave girl told him that he could be made well by going to visit Elisha. Make it memorable!

The most enjoyable drama is spontaneous and evokes participation by lots of people. In her youth, my mother and her cousins put on plays and even imaginary marching band drills for all the family members gathered. One of her uncles reciprocated by dressing up like a tramp and limping toward the children once when they were just out of sight of Grandma's farmhouse. They ran screaming to the house and right under the bed! The "tramp" followed them, laughing uncontrollably. Drama will give your family many wonderful memories, bringing communication alive!

STORYTELLING:
CAN YOU IMAGINE... CAN YOU CREATE?

Storytelling takes the products of our imagination and recreates them for the enjoyment of others. The latest research in education confirms what the Bible demonstrates: stories are the best way to transmit values from generation to generation. The Old Testament narrated history in a timeless manner. Jesus continued a long tradition through the use of parables. As a parent, your stories connect your child to the past, teach the difference between right and wrong, help him develop godly character, and affirm that life is an exciting process of observation, discovery and imagination.

In addition, stories will exercise your child's memory. Study of oral cultures shows that "uneducated" people without a written language are often able to perform prodigious feats of memory with ease. Yugoslavian bards, for instance, can listen to a thirty-minute-long story, told musically, and then repeat it thought for thought and nearly word for word. The same principles apply to children; even before your child is reading you can use storytelling to enhance both his imagination and his memory.

Storytelling is vital for life, and it can be easily taught with just a little fore-planning. We will spend a great deal of time in the "Project Pages" section of this book discussing

Even before he is reading, you can use storytelling with your child to enhance both his imagination and his memory.

different tactics for teaching storytelling to your children, but it is vital to note here that the way you tell stories to your child will enhance his own storytelling ability.

Here are three ideas to enhance storytelling:

1. **Create a storyteller's chair.** Professors Huckleberry and Strother suggest that with some tin foil or gold spray paint and some inexpensive red or purple velvet, you can create a throne of honor in which the storyteller may sit. What a fun way to spark a desire to exercise imagination and creativity!

2. **Debrief stories well.** Most parents read or invent stories for their children. Although I suggested earlier that you not go overboard in "analyzing" stories, there are a few elements, an understanding of which makes it possible for your child to weave exciting tales for himself. You can help your child become aware of what makes stories exciting by asking such questions as, "Is the writer just trying to entertain us, or is she saying something about people?" "What do you like about this story?" "What have you learned from this story?" "How does the author convey action and suspense?" "Is the story boring? Why?" As you ask your child what makes the story interesting, you can point out things such as the characters speaking in dialogue form, how the action progresses and other elements which will ultimately help him create more interesting stories himself. Again, as noted earlier, a good story does not consist of the structure that pulls it together. However, a basic understanding of structure makes story construction easier for your child.

3. **Infuse stories with emotion.** Emotion draws your child into the story, generating curiosity. It also sets a positive example of how to communicate in a way that interests others.

WE ARE MADE IN THE IMAGE OF A CREATIVE GOD

By now, you have access to a whole new repertoire of activities which you can work on with your child. When God created us in his image, he gave us the ability to use words to create. It is only fitting that we learn, and in turn teach our children, how to use this powerful gift as effectively as possible. The next chapter applies the lessons learned in the construction of the first four pillars to the area of poise, or how your child handles social situations in a way that demonstrates communication excellence.

CHAPTER NINE

HELPING YOUR CHILD DEVELOP POISE IN SOCIAL SITUATIONS

HAVE YOU EVER BEEN EMBARRASSED BY YOUR CHILD?

Every parent has a story about a time when they were mortified by the behavior of their child. Whether it is a shy child hiding *underneath* your dress at church in front of about 20 people, or a teenager, upon meeting someone you greatly respect, mumbling a surly greeting and barely offering a limp handshake while avoiding eye contact.

This chapter tackles the fifth pillar in our building of communication: poise. The material contained herein is wildly popular with audiences to whom I speak. People seem incredulous to discover that you can train a child to be polite, respectful, and even engaging! In this chapter, you will learn how to teach your child the most significant social skills: greeting people, maintaining a conversation, behaving in public, expressing appreciation, answering the telephone, and answering the door. But first, let's discuss why social skills are so vital to your child.

Studies

show that

attractiveness

has less to do

with physical

beauty than

with how

well one

communicates

with others.

THE BREATHTAKING SIGNIFICANCE
OF SOCIAL SKILLS

Speech links your child to his environment, bringing him into contact with others, and allowing him to learn and share ideas. Children who "link-up" effortlessly find it easier to relate to others, and therefore enjoy smoother social interaction. Even more significant, effective communication skills allow your child to influence, rather than be influenced by, the culture around him.

Most people assume that children excel in social skills because of physical attractiveness. Yet studies show that attractiveness has less to do with physical beauty than with how well one communicates with others. Professors Gottman, Gonso and Rasmussen studied the characteristics of popular children and discovered that children who know how to give and receive positive verbal reinforcement are popular with their peers and are better able to make friends. They can make contributions to conversation, exert influence, and be recognized in a social manner. Even as early as preschool, notes Professor Stohl, those who use communication skills to take charge of social situations become more noticeable to their peers, and are thus viewed as more attractive. In addition, a multitude of studies show that, unfair as it may seem, teachers spend more time with and give higher evaluations to children who communicate well.

Obviously, your child can benefit through stronger and smoother social skills. Most children, at one time or another, struggle with this. Some are too shy, and others are too hyperactive! Both of those responses, however, seem to originate in the same place, as we will now discuss.

THE FEAR OF THE UNKNOWN MAKES US UNCOMFORTABLE

The fear of not knowing what to do in social situations seems to be the single greatest culprit in children's lack of comfort in such situations. Entering a social situation with an adult may seem as intimidating to a child as if *you* were entering a social situation with a well-known public figure. The President of the United States, to avoid awkward situations when visiting with foreign dignitaries, retains a staff of dozens of experts trained in the "protocol" of various nations. These experts brief the President on how to greet a dignitary according to that person's customs, explain which gestures are not acceptable (in some countries the common American gesture signifying "Okay" by making a circle with the forefinger and thumb, is a vulgarity), demonstrate how to sit properly (in some Mid-Eastern countries, showing the bottom of one's shoe is an unforgivable insult), describe what might be served and how to eat it, and suggest what constitutes proper topics of conversation.

If you can gently instruct your child on *how* to act appropriately, he will feel more comfortable, and in my experience, will respond with more pleasing behavior. You can help your child overcome his fear of the unknown by practicing social skills in the home before actually trying them out. As a parent, you will have to think ahead, never assuming that your child automatically knows how to behave. Here are some ideas about instructing your child in common social situations.

HOW TO TEACH YOUR CHILD TO GREET OTHERS

Whether consciously or unconsciously, we view others based on first impressions. The first few seconds give us an impression that governs everything else we think about

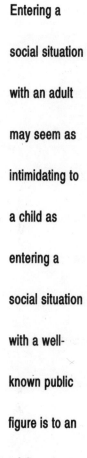

Entering a social situation with an adult may seem as intimidating to a child as entering a social situation with a well-known public figure is to an adult.

If you can

gently

instruct your

child on

how to act

appropriately,

he will feel

more

comfortable

and will

respond

with more

pleasing

behavior.

that person. In fact, that first impression can last in your mind for several years! Teaching appropriate greeting skills is easy, but getting your child to follow through will take some practice.

An effective greeting contains two steps: first, the introduction, and second, the conversation stimulant. Let's say you wish to introduce your son to Horace Englebert, an associate from work. You would first say, "Excuse me, Mr. Englebert, this is my son Junior. Junior, Mr. Englebert is one of the men with whom I work." Train your son to offer a firm (not crushing) handshake while looking your colleague in the eye, and saying, "Hello, Mr. Englebert, I am pleased to meet you." Second, it is appropriate for you to stimulate conversation between the two. "Junior, you might be very interested in Mr. Englebert's hobby of gluing toothpicks into eight-inch-tall statues of the Alamo." (Okay, okay, so this example is *extremely* hypothetical.) Or, you could say, "Mr. Englebert, since you appreciate fine talent, you would be interested to know that Junior is an accomplished pianist. Why, he just finished learning Opus 360 by Klaus Swindlepucker."

Here are some of the finer points of greetings:

- Your child should not assume that the other person remembers him. If he is greeting someone he has not seen for a while, teach your child to reintroduce himself and give the person a brief recap of where they last met. Your child should *never* put someone on the spot by saying, "Do you remember me?" or, "What's my name?"

- Help your child learn to make the other person as comfortable as possible. Simple, appropriate greetings may include:

"How are you today?"

"How is your family?" (Ask by name.) "What have you been doing lately?"

If the person is a public figure, or is otherwise not known to your child, coach your child to say something like:

"I am very pleased to meet you."

"I would like to know more about you (your work, your family, etc.)."

Do not ask questions which might be too personal or put the person on the spot.

Help your child learn to disengage from the conversation when it is time to go. Except in extreme circumstances, it is polite to wait until the conversation seems to be near an end, extend your hand again, look the person in the eye, and say, "I am pleased to have met you," and then offer a pleasant goodbye such as, "Enjoy the rest of your day," or, "Have a wonderful day." If the person is long-winded and your child really needs to go, he can say, "I'm sorry, it is time for me to go," and offer his goodbye. Teach your child to offer a reason if possible, but never to lie. Good reasons would be things like, "I told my parents I would meet them at 12:30, and I have just enough time to get there" or, "I'm working right now so I must get back to the task at hand."

HOW TO TEACH APPROPRIATE PUBLIC BEHAVIOR

It is vitally important to coach your child on what constitutes appropriate behavior in a public setting. Do not

The first few seconds give us an impression that governs everything else we think about that person. In fact, that first impression can last for several years!

assume that he knows what to do. The importance of this kind of training is highlighted in Caryl Waller Krueger's practical, idea-filled book, *Six Weeks to Better Parenting* (Pelican Press). Mrs. Krueger's advice is so common sense that it ought to be obvious. However, for most people, it is far from obvious. I once saw a young boy run up to a male adult speaker and punch him *in the groin*. He meant it as a gesture of play, I'm sure, but his mother nearly fainted dead away (and so did the speaker, by the way)! In turn, the mother nearly extinguished the life of the young boy, who, bewildered, failed to recognize that he had done anything inappropriate. The whole situation could have been avoided had he been coached in appropriate behavior in advance. On the other hand, I know a mother who *always* coaches her young son, even before something as routine as a church service. I have heard many people comment on that boy's incredibly polite behavior, never realizing that it is far from accidental. Such behavior may be attributed to the child, but reflects nicely on the parents, too!

VISITING

Your child will benefit from opportunities to visit with adults, and you can manufacture situations in which to give him practice. For example, the next time you go to church, require your child to greet one or two adults and engage them in a conversation for at least one minute. It may seem artificial at first, but who knows? Maybe the conversation will last even longer. The child may even enjoy it. He will certainly learn from it! Afterwards, debrief the experience over dinner and praise your child for his efforts. Point out how special people feel when others acknowledge and appreciate their presence.

One of the objects of teaching visiting skills, at least initially, is to make your child feel comfortable. Practice visiting skills with guests in your own home first, where children feel more comfortable. Then move on to visits outside the home, brief ones at first—30 minutes or less. Mrs. Krueger suggests explaining the purpose of the visit and reviewing appropriate behavior before each visit. How should this person be greeted? If he or she is a close friend or relative, a kiss or hug may be more appropriate than a handshake. How should your child respond to an offer of food? How does he ask to use the rest room? How should he ask if he wants to play with the toys in the other room?

Another way to put your child at ease is for him to take something to share with the person being visited. A game, picture, small book, or snack are all appropriate. This puts the child on familiar turf in an unfamiliar place. Also, for every rule about what the child cannot do on the visit, think of a privilege which the child *can* exercise. At the end of the visit, debrief. Praise your child for good behavior and manners, discuss whether the purpose of the visit was achieved, and help him become satisfied with the results.

CONVERSATION WITH ADULTS

Ability to converse with adults is a mark of maturity in children. You can enhance your child's maturity by equipping him with strategies for difficult situations. Children often fall apart in conversation because they feel they have nothing valuable to say.

It is perfectly appropriate to prepare your child for specific situations. At a birthday party, make sure your child knows how to respond when given a gift. He should be able to say more than just "thank you," and should know how to respond when he receives a duplicate gift. The response should be gracious and appropriate (not, "Did you keep the receipt?").

Those who

make a habit

of blessing

other people

will find a

significant

mission field

right before

their very

eyes.

Your child will become more comfortable in social situations *outside* the home if you converse frequently *inside* your home. One excellent book which can help you converse with your child is Dr. Jane M. Healy's *How to Have Intelligent and Creative Conversations with Your Kids* (Doubleday). Dr. Healy suggests dozens of playful topics for conversation. Here are some of them for each age group:

PRIMARY LEVEL (3-7):

If you could spend one day as an animal, which one would you choose to be? Tell about what you think your day might be like.

How can you tell if someone is your friend? What do you need to do to be a friend?

What if you found a secret passage in your house or apartment?

MIDDLE LEVEL (8-12):

If you were asked to invent a new holiday, what would it be for? What would you call it? When and how would it be celebrated?

Pretend there is a robot standing in the room. What would you have to change about it so that you could call it human?

You have been invited to participate in an experiment with a newly developed time machine. You may choose to go forward or backward in time to any place you wish. Would you go? If so, what year or period would you like to land in? Why?

UPPER LEVEL (13 AND UP):

Pretend you leave your bedroom one morning and close the door. Is your bed still there if no one can see it, touch it, or sense it in any other way? How could you prove it?

How might the course of human civilization have been different if people did not need to eat but could absorb all the nourishment they needed from air and water?

How is a game of football like the United States government?

You can probably think of other fun topics of conversation to use with your child and for your child to use with others. Topics such as these help acclimate him to the flow and pace of conversation.

EXPRESSING APPRECIATION

Poised people know how to express appreciation to others for their kindness. Bennett Cerf offered the following advice:

> A very wise public-relations counsel cautions letter writers to delete the pronoun "I" as much as possible. "A weekend thank-you note that opens 'I had a wonderful time,'" he points out, "is not half so captivating as one beginning, 'You are a wonderful hostess.' Both say 'thank you,' but, ah, my friends, the second is the one that will get you asked back!"

As Christians, our purpose is not so much to get asked back, but to love others. The Bible commands us to encourage one another in the faith, spur one another on to good deeds, and love our neighbor as ourselves. Those who make a habit of blessing other people will find a significant

Taught

properly,

young

children

enjoy

answering

the telephone

and will take

a great deal

of pride in

doing so.

mission field right before their very eyes. Your child can participate in this blessing as part of his developing communication ability.

ANSWERING THE TELEPHONE

Explain to your child that answering the telephone provides the opportunity to make an impression on someone, either negative or positive. Teach him to use a pleasant voice, inquire about the caller, and take messages. Have your child practice on a toy telephone to prove he can do it correctly.

I rediscovered the importance of telephone manners through a conversation with a four-year-old, home-school child named Kyle. I telephoned his family in reference to an upcoming conference, and the following conversation took place when Kyle answered the telephone:

"Smith residence, this is Kyle," he said distinctly. "Who would you like to speak to?"

"Hello," I said, taken aback, "I would like to speak to your father."

"My father is not available," replied young Kyle. "Would you like to speak to my mother?"

I said, "That would be fine."

"May I ask who's calling?" he inquired.

Caught off guard once again, I said, "Yes, this is Jeff," not bothering to overload him with additional information such as my last name.

"Hold one moment, please," he said, and dashed off. Then I heard him say, "Mom, there is a Jeff on the phone for you. He did not say what kind of Jeff he was!"

You can bet that I was impressed with the poise and skill that little Kyle demonstrated when answering the phone, and a little embarrassed that I underestimated his talent at doing so. Because I was impressed, my whole approach to Kyle changed, and our interaction rose to a new level. Both of us benefitted.

When teaching your child to answer the telephone, keep security concerns in mind. In our insecure and some-times dangerous world, it may be best for your child to not answer the telephone in your absence. If he must, teach him how to answer without indicating that you are gone. A proper response might be, "My mother cannot come to the telephone right now. May I take a message?" Be sure mes-sage paper and a pen are handy. Teach him to ask for the name, proper spelling, telephone number, and what the call is regarding, as appropriate. Designate a standard place where family members can pick up and leave messages. If you *are* home, but not available, saying, "My mother can-not come to the telephone right now. May I take a mes-sage?" will suffice. One young boy with whom I spoke indicated, much to his mother's embarrassment, that his mother was on the toilet right then and couldn't come to the phone!

Think of various situations your child might encounter on the telephone, and then test him once or twice by call-ing from a pay phone. Devise a reward system for proper responses to these surprise calls. Taught properly, young children enjoy answering the telephone and will take a great deal of pride in doing so. In return for answering pleasantly and appropriately, give your child the privilege of making telephone calls. Be sure to set up clear rules about what times of the day he may receive calls, how long the calls may be, and whether he needs to ask permission.

ANSWERING THE DOOR

Answering the door is good practice for greeting others. The rules will differ from home to home depending on how safe your neighborhood is and whether the child can view the caller through the door. Teach your child to ask who it is before unlocking and opening the door. Clarify the rules as to who is to be let in; it is rude to leave friends and family standing outside, but it is perfectly appropriate for strangers. If the caller is unknown, your child should ask, "May I tell my parents who is here?" Again, in our sad days of high crime rates, it may be best for your children not to answer the door at all when you are not home.

REWARDING ENTHUSIASM

Sometimes your child's enthusiasm may cause a mix-up. When he was six or seven years of age, my brother Tim once answered the door with his telephone greeting: "Hello, Myers residence." It is still an embarrassment to him many years later. Mix-ups are no big deal; they are part of learning. The skills your child can learn by completing these simple tasks, however, allow him to develop poise and confidence, and leave a positive first impression that can benefit him and encourage others for years to come.

CHAPTER TEN

HELPING YOUR CHILD RELATE TO OTHERS: A LIFE SKILL

EMPATHY: A CHARACTER QUALITY OF CHRIST

Communication brings your child in contact with others, allowing him to listen, learn, and mature into a more well-rounded human being. It also gives him the opportunity to encourage others, contributing fullness and meaning to their lives. This ability to understand others and relate to their lives is called *empathy*. It forms the basis for the sixth and final pillar in the building of communication. Empathy means the ability to relate to others in such a way as to ensure that they know we really understand them. Empathy is the apex of all communication skill since it makes our relationships and impact on the world meaningful.

Empathy is a quality displayed by Jesus in relation to us:

Since the children have flesh and blood, he too shared in their humanity so that by his death he might destroy him who holds the power of death— that is, the devil—and free those who all their lives were held in slavery by their fear of death...

Empathy: the ability to understand others and relate to their lives.

Empathy

shows the

other person

that you

understand,

not necessarily

that you

agree.

For this reason he had to be made like his brothers in every way, in order that he might become a merciful and faithful high priest in service to God, and that he might make atonement for the sins of the people. Because he himself suffered when he was tempted, he is able to help those who are being tempted (Hebrews 2:14-18, NIV).

Jesus identified with our sufferings in part because he had suffered. Even though we may not have been through the same experiences as those around us, we should attempt to *identify* with them so we can more effectively *reach* them. To empathize does not mean the same thing as sympathize, which connotes more of a "feeling sorry for" or endorsing the beliefs, attitudes and values of others. Empathy shows the other person that you understand, not necessarily that you agree.

Two primary ways to develop the communication skill of empathy include active listening and advanced conversation ability.

How to Teach Active Listening to Your Child

King Solomon, the world's wisest man, warned in Proverbs 1:32-33, "For the waywardness of the simple will kill them, and the complacency of fools will destroy them; but whoever *listens* to [wisdom] will live in safety and be at ease, without fear of harm" (NIV). James 1:19 says, "Everyone should be quick to listen, slow to speak, and slow to become angry" (NIV). Proverbs 1:5 says, "Let the wise listen and add to their learning" (NIV). The Bible also calls those who do not listen fools.

Active listening occurs when the listener concentrates on feeling the emotion behind what the speaker says. Active listening requires the listener to overcome tiredness, to avoid preoccupation with other thoughts, to not get ahead of the speaker, and to avoid mentally formulating a response before the speaker is finished.

Practice active listening before teaching it to your child. When your child has something to say, stop what you are doing, get on his level, look him in the eye, and treat what he says as important by smiling, nodding and asking questions.

Active listening also means listening to *comprehend*. An active listener understands the central idea being expressed, identifies the arguments in support of that idea, and figures out what the *speaker* thinks is important. Every child can learn to comprehend the central idea expressed in conversation, or even in books, stories, movies and news items. Practice by giving your child the opportunity to listen to a speaker, story or song, and then testing him through a true/false quiz. For added realism, include *noise*, making it difficult to concentrate.

Here are the six steps to active listening:

1. **Be attentive.** Demonstrate attentiveness by looking the person in the eye, and sitting up straight. Lean forward instead of slouching, and uncross your arms to take a more open stance. Nod and smile when appropriate.

2. **Show interest.** Keep the discussion going with verbal responses such as, "I see," "Uh-huh," and "Yes, go on."

3. **Reflect back.** When the person pauses for a response, reflect his feelings back so he can hear them voiced. This convinces him that you are listening. You can reflect either the content or feelings the person is expressing. If the topic is emotional in nature, consider the person's feelings first. Common reflecting sentences include:

Active listening occurs when the listener concentrates on feeling the emotion behind what the speaker says.

We model

one-way

communication

to our children

by avoiding

personal

involvement.

- "Wow, it sounds like you're really…"

- "I hear how you feel."

- "If I'm hearing you correctly…"

4. Clarify. Question the statement until the person agrees that you understand fully.

- "Let me restate what you've said to make sure I understand."

- "Is there something else?"

- "Is the problem _____?"

5. Re-state everything. Especially in complex conversation, with difficult to understand material, it is important to make sure you are on the same wavelength.

- "If I understand you, you plan to _____."

- "Let me see if I understand the reasons for what you want to do…"

6. Summarize. Put together the essential facts and ideas.

HOW TO TEACH CONVERSATION SKILLS TO YOUR CHILD

Conversation may be a lost art in our nation. Most people would rather *watch* something than engage in a social situation where the focus of attention is *each other*. We expect children to play with other children and leave adults alone. We model one-way communication to our children by avoiding personal involvement. One study showed that 94% of all questions refer to the immediate situation, reflecting on such valueless topics as the weather.

Fortunately, there are ways to solve this problem. Here are some unique approaches:

1. **Use a tennis ball to reinforce the importance of conversation.** The speaker holds a tennis ball while speaking, throwing it to someone else when finished. The second person says something and then throws the ball to someone else. Try this with your child to demonstrate the flow of conversation.

2. **"Prime" the pump.** Give your child conversation tips before going into unfamiliar territory. I travel several days each month, frequently meeting new people. I am always grateful to hosts who brief me about those whom we will be meeting. It makes conversation easier, allowing us to "hit it off" almost immediately. Your child will benefit from similar preparation. If you know with whom your child will be visiting, hint at possible topics of conversation. For instance, "What kind of dog is Sammy?" "Are you a war veteran?" or, "Did you remodel this room yourself?"

3. **Think of five topics.** Have your child think of five topics he would like to discuss with any given adult: his new bicycle, a current event, what he is learning in school, or a question about a sports team.

4. **Think of five questions.** Alter the "five topics" strategy for older children. At a retirement center, for instance, he may think of questions such as, "What was it like to live during the Great Depression?" "Will you tell me about your family?" "What is something that one of your children has done of which you are proud?" or, "What are some of your fond memories of childhood?" Usually, one of these topics sparks an interest, giving your child the chance to hear and appreciate history through the words of an older person.

Asking

questions is

perhaps the

most

effective

stimulus of

good

conversation.

Here are some questions to use in other situations:

Tell me about…

…where you grew up.

…a favorite childhood memory.

…a good book you have read recently.

…one thing you would attempt if you knew you could not fail.

…an exciting place you have been.

- Describe your dream vacation.

- What is your favorite meal? Animal? Place in the world?

- If you could do one thing to change the world, what would you do?

- Describe the most adventurous thing you have ever done.

- Some people consider themselves to be introverts and some consider themselves to be extroverts. Which do you think you are and why?

- What is your hobby or what do you enjoy spending time on?

- If you could build your very own dream house, what would you put in it?

Asking questions is perhaps the most effective stimulus of good conversation. Moreover, it leaves a positive impression in the mind of the other person. I'll never forget my college roommate returning from a date exclaiming, "That was the most brilliant girl I have ever dated!" When I asked what gave him that impression, he could not think of an answer. It turned out, of course, that *she* asked *him* lots of questions, so he talked about himself the whole evening, coming away with the impression that *she* was brilliant!

EMPATHY: MISSION IMPOSSIBLE?

Empathy is a communication skill in great demand. We talk but we do not really know how to empathize with one another. An eerie, uncomfortable silence has developed in our souls. Learning to listen and converse is important to fulfilling our mission on earth of reaching, touching and loving others as God loves us. If you and your family embrace this mission, your influence on this world will be far-reaching and profound.

Now that we have covered the foundation and all six pillars of communication success, it is time to begin building the roof! The next part of the book gives you hundreds of exciting communication-building ideas for children of all age ranges. It is time to get practical!

Learning to listen and converse is important to fulfilling our mission on earth of reaching, touching and loving others as God loves us.

CHAPTER ELEVEN

COMMUNICATION-BUILDING ACTIVITIES FOR EVERY CHILD

NOW IT'S TIME TO "GET PRACTICAL"

The first part of this book offered dozens of ideas for improving the quality of communication in your family. This last section offers dozens more in the form of specific projects you can use to work on particular communication skills. Each project is tailored to a specific age group and categorized as to which communication skill it develops.

HERE'S HOW!

Each project from age three and up is organized to maximize its usefulness. Here is an overview of how the projects are structured:

Project Sketch gives you an overview of each project.

How-To shows you what materials are needed and how to accomplish the project successfully.

Timely Tip provides special insight into field-tested ways to get the most out of each project.

Future Adventure offers variations of the project so that you can extend the life of those which work best for you.

Make it Memorable shows you a relationship-building key to each project that makes it something your child will never forget!

IDEAS THAT WORK—FROM PLAYPEN TO PODIUM

In addition to being highly practical, each project is "age integrated" to work on skills specific to each developmental level. The projects are divided into sections as follows:

Infants: Communication with infants is extremely important; your child is born ready to communicate, and most of the "landmarks" in communication training have passed by three years of age! This section gives you 14 practical ideas you can start using right now, or give to a friend who has a baby.

Toddlers: Toddlers are human sponges. They absorb everything—especially communication. This chapter shows you how to take advantage of your child's natural inquisitiveness to stimulate his communication ability.

Ages Three to Seven: This is the age at which communication-building becomes really fun! You can create a desire for communication in your child through play activities, and this chapter shows you how. It also gives more ways to encourage storytelling than you probably have ever seen in one place!

Ages Eight to Twelve: During the pre-teen years, children can learn how to be confident in social situations and begin to learn basic speech skills.

This chapter starts at the very beginning, using creative ideas to make communication development fun.

Ages Thirteen and Up: This is the age at which young people have the opportunity to work on the leadership and communication skills they will use throughout life. In this chapter they will learn skills of critical inquiry, interviewing and listening, as well as different kinds of speeches that even the most shy teenager can accomplish.

Use these projects to their fullest potential by adding your own comments and variations on the blank "Notes" pages you will find throughout.

HOW TO TARGET SPECIFIC SKILL NEEDS

Finally, each project is geared toward practicing some of the specific skills we discussed in the first section of the book: strengthening your child's sense of purpose, becoming more aware of the world around, becoming a better learner, thinking more creatively, developing poise, and relating to others. Each project is tagged with a primary and a secondary skill target. To review, here are the tags you will see for each skill:

Purpose

Purpose results from a child's recognition of his parents' love, as well as a sense of the excitement and meaning of everyday life. It supports communication excellence by taking away fear and making your child's communication appealing to others. In turn, communication excellence generates enthusiasm for other areas of your child's life.

Awareness

Awareness results from a child's curiosity about the world, and it supports communication excellence by giving your child the ability to become more aware of the experiences of others, how to reach the heart of an audience, and how to effectively translate his own experiences into meaningful information for an audience.

Learning

Learning results from a child's love of gaining new information, and it supports communication excellence by giving your child a base of experience from which to speak. In turn, communication excellence generates a heightened sense of the importance of words, making a deeper level of expression possible.

Creative Thinking

Creative Thinking results from experiences which allow your child to be creative and to think in interesting, exciting ways. It supports communication excellence by giving your child a unique, exciting perspective on life, spurring him on to a new level of quick, powerful thinking.

Poise

Poise results from a child learning to be comfortable in a wide variety of settings. It raises your child's comfort level and skill in front of an audience or in any social situation in which he might find himself.

Empathy

Empathy results from a child being trained to listen to and learn from the experiences of others. It improves your child's skill at relating to others, increasing his attractiveness to them and thus the power of his message.

Now It Starts...

Please allow me to make a personal note here. The Apostle Paul says that we must be prepared to communicate with others in a gentle and respectful fashion, taking care that our speech is "seasoned with salt" (Colossians 4:6, NIV). Salt is both a preservative and a healing agent. In the same way, communication preserves and builds fragile human relationships.

I see these projects as more than just fun things to do with your child. They form the bedrock of his social impact on the world, showing him how to "salt" others in a way that causes them to grow and become what God wants them to be.

Each human being is made in the image of God, and we will all have to give account someday for how we bore that image. Yet, most people are terrified of communicating publicly. In one survey, adults listed "Speaking before a group" as their number one fear. It was named more often than financial problems, illness, and even death!

These projects will equip your child to take the higher ground, persevering where you might shrink in fear. Ultimately, young people who learn to communicate, and to do so truthfully and lovingly, will become the next generation of leaders. My prayer is that your child will be among them.

CHAPTER TWELVE

INFANT COMMUNICATION

COMMUNICATION:
A BREATH OF LIFE FOR YOUR BABY

Most people seem surprised to discover that how you communicate with your infant may have a long-term impact on his communication development, but it is true. This is not to say that a parent's influence at this age level is fully understood because it is not, even by researchers who have studied parents and children for decades. But researchers now recognize that infant communication is extremely important, and that infants do have the awareness and intelligence to process words and emotions.

A striking example of the horrible consequences of the old philosophy, that infant communication was irrelevant, was discovered in the ruins of the communist regime in Romania. Relief workers discovered thousands of small children who had been forcibly taken from their parents and raised by the government, some of whom were as old as five years, yet were the size and maturity level of infants. These children had been kept in large rooms full of dozens of cribs, with just enough nursing care to feed and sometimes clothe them, but not to communicate with or mother them. These poor children could not care for themselves or talk, and many experts wondered if they would ever be able to take a normal role in society. Clinging desperately to

Babies not only

attempt to

speak, they

actually mimic

the "turn-taking"

which is

necessary for

conversation.

their rescuers, these children experienced love, cuddling and communication for the first time in their short lives. Thankfully, most have been adopted into loving homes, providing the opportunity for somewhat normal development.

This chapter is not designed to teach you how to communicate with your baby—that comes naturally. However, it *will* enhance your ability to understand your baby's stages of communication development and deepen your ability to build a strong foundation for his future communication skills. As with all teaching tools, "balance" is very important. Chattering to your baby all the time, or creating "flash cards" and language drills would quickly become counterproductive! This chapter will help clarify what is appropriate and healthy.

HOW IMPORTANT IS COMMUNICATION WITH YOUR BABY?

Oddly enough, the word infant literally comes from the Latin word "in" (meaning without) and "fan" (meaning to speak). It literally means "without speech." We now know that even though the physical structures for actual speech are not in place, your baby is trying out his inborn ability to speak from day one! According to Dr. Rachel Stark, an infant researcher, many of those who have studied each stage of speech development have concluded that infant vocalization is actually an attempt to mimic human speech. Moreover, according to Dr. Stark, babies not only attempt to speak, they actually mimic the "turn-taking" which is necessary for conversation.

Additionally, infants are sensitive to the communication of others from birth. According to Professor Baltaxe, another infant researcher, babies react to the quality of feelings expressed in the voice and can even discern emotions in the voice and match them to facial expressions. Most infants desire communication so strongly that they are more interested in the sound of adult voices than any other sound, including instrumental music.

When our son Graham was born, Danielle and I put this theory to the test. We talked to Graham as if he were going to respond, even when he was just a few weeks old. It often felt silly to carry on "conversation" with a pre-verbal infant, but we were rewarded when his eyes flashed, legs kicked, and his tiny mouth moved producing noises that would someday become speech. He loved it! And so did we.

It is no surprise that experts now consider infancy a crucial time for gaining the ability to use language effectively. Dr. William Fowler of the Center for Early Learning and Child Care in Cambridge, Massachusetts, a researcher of infant/parent interactions, concluded that parents who focus on speech early in the life of a child will enhance his chances of becoming a better communicator later in life. In fact, dozens of studies show that the mother's talk with her infant is the most significant factor in the later ability of the child to communicate.

How is this so? Dr. Carol Gibb Harding explains that mothers guess what the child's communication means and react in a certain way. Through this response, the infant becomes aware of the connection between its behavior and the mother's. As the infant starts to communicate, the mother "ups the ante," requiring ever more advanced communication. In this way, the mother demonstrates to the child the importance of communication. This phenomenon is called "motherese."

In order to begin putting this knowledge into practice, it might be helpful to know a little bit about your baby's stages of communication development.

A mother's talk with her infant is the most significant factor in the later ability of the child to communicate.

Children

understand

before they *act.*

Just as adults .

can understand

more than they

can explain,

babies

understand

words before

their vocal

structures allow

them to

reproduce

those words.

Getting to Know Your Baby

Even before they learn to speak, children communicate through gaze direction, eye contact, vocalizing, and reaching and pointing, whether or not they do this with the *intention* of communicating. Speech emerges through the course of time in a predictable pattern, though the *pace* will differ for each child. Understanding these patterns will help you become aware of normal development. It will also help you enjoy your child's growth more, since you will notice his passing from one stage to the next!

If your child is dramatically behind, you may wish to discuss the problem with your physician. Otherwise, just be sure you are creating a stimulating environment for your child, and be patient! A friend of mine did not speak, according to his mother, a single word until he was three years of age. Today he is a brilliant writer and gifted novelist.

Keep in mind that at every stage, children *understand* before they do. Just as adults can usually understand more than they can explain, babies understand words before their vocal structures allow them to reproduce those words. With that in mind, here are the major stages of infant speech development.

Stage One: Vocalization

Vocalization starts immediately at birth. Cooing sounds, or "oohs and ahs," appear during the first and second months, and babbling ensues at about three months. Babbling usually is a consonant sound repeated over and over again such as "ba-ba-ba." Despite the hopes of many a proud father, the baby is not likely to say "pa-pa" with meaningful intent until much later!

STAGE TWO: LALLING

Lalling is a sound that the child makes, likes and repeats. This stage usually begins at about six months of age. Somewhere between the babbling stage and the lalling stage you will notice your baby using his voice as he attempts to manipulate the objects he is playing with. The best explanation for this phenomenon is that your baby is "representing the objects" to himself, describing to himself what they are and what they mean. It is hard to say whether he is really thinking about them, or is just connecting the need to use his voice in response to the world around.

STAGE THREE: ECHOLALIA

Echolalia comes from the word "echo" (to repeat) and "lalia" (speech), meaning "repeating what others say." Echolalia begins at about nine or ten months of age. At this point your child begins devising "fast maps," or rough meanings of words which serve as temporary definitions to use until he is sure of the meaning. You can expect your baby to *understand* certain words at this age (such as "no"). At about eleven months he may actually begin using words with meaning, although the words will be more clear to Mom and Dad or older siblings, who are able to make an immediate connection between the words used and what he wants.

STAGE FOUR: JARGONING

At the jargoning stage, your child may look at you and rattle off a word or several words which you do not understand. Jargoning will occur sometime after echolalia, although the length of the time is different for each child. Children who are more physically active are less likely to speak, while those who do not express as much physical activity may develop more quickly in that area. Jargoning is sometimes called "prattling" or "baby talk." It actually has the rhythm of speech, although few words will make sense to adults.

The best way to make these words clearer is by trying to guess what your child is saying. Caution: this stage may require a great deal of patience as you gradually learn to interpret the words used. It is best not to scold or correct the child for the inaccurate use of a word. Instead, just keep saying the correct pronunciation. If the baby says "gamma," you say "grandma." Studies consistently demonstrate that your child will learn how to pronounce words from your use of correct pronunciation.

STAGE FIVE: SENTENCES

The final stage is the use of *sentences*. Most children begin using simple sentences at about 18 months of age. At first, these sentences are for the purpose of requesting information or objects, such as "What that?" or "Give ball." Eventually, the child begins making statements about the world such as "That dog," or "Ball on chair." His language system will become more sophisticated, yet growth may come rapidly at times and very slowly at others. Language learning is like a volcano; just because there is no smoke does not mean it is extinct! It may brew and stew and steam and build up pressure for quite a while before erupting! Often children go for days or weeks without any visible signs of speech development, and then "boom"—your ears hardly have time for a rest.

Understanding these five stages will help you track the development of your child. Next we will apply all of this theory and make it eminently practical through fourteen powerful, practical ideas.

FOURTEEN POWERFUL IDEAS
YOU CAN USE RIGHT NOW

Recent studies have shown, noted one reporter, that babies are, in fact, human! As awkward as it seems to talk to a child who cannot respond, you must make a conscious effort to be verbal around your baby. Mem Fox explains that children "learn to read by reading. They learn to write by writing. And they learn to talk by talking." Here are some helpful suggestions:

ONE: TALK TO YOUR BABY!

Remember, you're the best teacher your child will ever have. You can talk about anything. Even talking aloud about whatever is on your mind will give your baby a model of speech. When putting away the dishes, talk about where the dishes go. When reading the sports page, talk about how your favorite team is doing and why. It is your voice, rather than the words you say, that matter most at this age.

To model this, we talk with our children about everything: what we were wearing, how to get dressed, our plans for the day, etc., and marvel at how intensely they seem to listen. Your voice is music to your child's ears!

Keep in mind that babies can pick up on emotional states, so be careful what you say and how you say it! Set a good example by not using baby talk. Your baby will appreciate a pleasant adult voice much more.

Another way to share talk with your baby is to whisper lightly in his ear or right next to his ear. He will listen intently to this very personal form of communication.

Once again, strive for a healthy balance. Don't try to keep up a constant chatter. *Share conversation* with your baby, treating everything he says as if it were actual speech.

Always respond

to whatever

your child looks

at or feels by

making it a

"teachable

moment."

TWO: PRACTICE TURN-TAKING

As you talk to your baby, pretend that you are having a conversation. If he gurgles or coos, act as if it represents a question or an answer to *your* question. To the observer, it seems quite strange, but by doing so, you encourage your baby to interact, thus drawing communication out of him. How do you do it? Make eye contact and just *talk*. If he grabs his foot, say "Yes, here's your foot." As Barbara Beckwith suggests, "Always respond to whatever your child looks at or feels by making it a 'teachable moment.'" At this level, the fact that you are taking turns is more important than *what* you say. For example:

Baby: "Ehh."

You: "Yes! I did notice that it is a beautiful day outside. What are you planning to do on such a beautiful day?"

Baby: "Ba, ba, ba, ba."

You: "Well! Such big plans for such a little tyke! I suppose we had better get you dressed and ready then, hmmm?"

Baby: "Ehh."

Be creative! Your baby is hearing your voice and recognizing that his vocalizations are meaningful to you. Maybe you could use this time to practice making up stories for when your baby reaches toddler age!

THREE: TALK WITH OTHER CHILDREN

Include your baby in conversation with others, especially with his siblings or other children. This provides "competition" in which the infant vies for attention. Human beings use communication to establish themselves in relationship to each other. Including an infant in conversation helps him learn to communicate in a real-world context.

FOUR: ASK LOTS OF QUESTIONS!

Asking lots of questions of your baby actually demonstrates to him that you are interested in conversation. According to Dr. Catherine Snow, one of the top experts in the world on infant communication development, such conversation with your child, even when he can't respond, helps him develop a sense of the "structure" of communication for later years when he can respond.

Here are some examples of how to ask questions of your baby:

- It's really a pretty day outside, hmm?

- That's a pretty color, isn't it?

- Oh, can you tell me more about your opinions on that issue?

- Oh my, we're feeling a little fussy, are we?

Any question that "passes the turn" to your baby, even though you know full well he cannot respond, is a great way to develop a strong foundation for future communication skill.

"Wh" questions, those which ask *what* and *where*, are also excellent:

- What is that? Can you say bird?

- Where did the ball go?

FIVE: SCHEDULE TIME WITH OTHER SIBLINGS

Teach your baby's older siblings, if he has any, how to communicate around him. Babies learn a great deal from older siblings about how to communicate effectively. Studies between older and younger children showed that older siblings who spent time with the baby, and were not physically aggressive with him, were more likely to be imitated by the baby and to be received by him in a friendly way.

Here are some things that older siblings can do to develop this kind of relationship with the baby:

- Imitate him when he makes sounds or kicks or moves his body.

- Start games with the baby, such as peek-a-boo.

- Help wash the baby.

- Feed the baby.

- Brush the baby's hair.

- Show toys to the baby.

SIX: IMITATE YOUR BABY

Strangely, babies pay special attention to mothers when mothers imitate an act they have just performed. Somehow, babies recognize that their movements and gurglings and smiles communicate. Even if it seems silly, when the baby throws his arms and legs in the air and makes exclamatory noises, imitate him by throwing your arms in the air and repeating the sound.

SEVEN: REPEAT YOURSELF

According to Professors Jones and Adamson, babies learn words when they hear them used over and over in a variety of contexts, so do not be afraid of repeating yourself in talking to your baby. For example: "Oh, Keisha! My little Keisha! Would you like to take a bath right now? Bath? How about a bath to wash you all up?"

EIGHT: READ TO YOUR BABY

Read aloud when your baby is in the room. Read the Bible, a children's book, or anything in which you are interested. Reading will help your baby adjust to the rhythm of speech.

NINE: LEAD IN COMMUNICATION

Draw your child into communication by encouraging him to be verbal about what he wants. If he gestures and grunts for a bite of applesauce, ask, "What do you want? *Applesauce?* Tell me, so I can give it to you." Ask "Yes?" while nodding your head or "No?" while shaking it. Sometimes he will be able to do so, sometimes not. With patience, you will elicit clearer responses from your child.

TEN: SHARE INITIATION OF CONVERSATION

In addition to asking questions, some experts suggest that you gradually begin to ignore grunts, and require some sort of verbalization before you respond to your baby's needs. One study reported by Dr. Harding showed that the most communicatively advanced infants were those whose mothers initiated less *than half* of the interactions. The most advanced infants learned to initiate "conversation." This means that you don't have to be the first to start conversation with your

One way to spur your child's communicative development is to gradually begin ignoring grunts, and to require some sort of verbalization before you respond to your baby's needs.

baby. Every once in a while let *him* make conversational noises or attempt to initiate conversation with *you*.

ELEVEN: TAKE NAMING WALKS

Carry your baby around the home, pointing out objects. As you name them, put action into the sentence such as "Shari likes to touch the pillow." Name the objects consistently; don't say "dog" one day and "pet" the next. Add complexity by noting the size and shape of the object. As she gets older, add more descriptive adjectives.

TWELVE: PLAY SIMPLE GAMES

Simple games that include conversation are always enjoyed by babies. "This little piggy went to market" or "Peek-a-boo," spoken in a playful, sing-song voice, will entertain your baby again and again. This kind of game can be repeated as long as your baby is responsive. Games do not have to be complex to be entertaining. You might simply hide an object such as a pacifier in your hand, and ask, "Where is the pacifier?" Let your baby pull your hand away, and then acknowledge the object. Dr. Jerome Bruner maintains that games such as these are like miniature conversations, reinforcing the structure of conversation.

THIRTEEN: USE RHYTHM AND MUSIC

Rhymes and soothing music have a rhythm that have an effect on the level of spontaneous activity in the brain. According to Dr. Frank E. X. Dance, an expert on the origin of speech, the spontaneous activity promoted by rhymes and music helps organize the brain, preparing it for the rhythm of speech. Take advantage of this fact by playing music regularly, reading rhyming books and dancing to music while holding your baby.

FOURTEEN: MAINTAIN EYE CONTACT

It has been said that the eye is the gateway to the soul. Make eye contact with your baby and respond to eye contact which he initiates, even when it isn't accompanied by vocal sounds. Ignore the old wives' tale that babies go cross-eyed if you put your face or objects too close. Get close to your baby, smile at him, and allow him to get to know more about being human from the one person who can best teach him—you.

WHERE TO GET MORE INFORMATION

These fourteen ideas will help you get started on a higher level of communication with your baby. However, they are just a start. I suggest scouring used bookstores for children's books and audio tapes which would be appropriate for your baby. Many libraries have resources on infant care which you might find helpful. Many shopping centers I have visited lately also have children's learning stores with educational toys and games. Make use of these resources. Few parents think twice about buying stimulating toys and games for toddlers and older children. Don't wait until then! Start now, while your child is still an infant. It may make a dramatic difference in his life.

As we will see in the next chapter, communication development can be accelerated as your child develops more complex language skills in what is commonly referred to as the toddler stage.

CHAPTER THIRTEEN

TODDLER COMMUNICATION

THE EXCITING NEW WORLD OF TODDLERHOOD

A toddler is like a human sponge; he is constantly soaking up information through his five senses. He wants to see, hear, taste, smell and touch everything—especially touch. Who can blame him? Each experience is a world-class event to those for whom it is utterly new.

Most adults remember their own toddlerhood dimly, if at all. As I prepared to write this chapter, I struggled with how to *describe* something in the way a toddler might experience it, as a means of conveying the intensity of this period of life. Some of my memories from toddlerhood are especially vivid, so I'll describe one of my own. It was at a carnival. If I close my eyes, the wonder of it returns: the smell of caramel corn and greasy fried cakes...diesel engines chugging and the squeak of the carousel as it grinds to a halt and delivers an endless stream of beaming adults and children...screams of delight whirling around...music soliciting me from five different places at once clashing in a cacophony of sound that makes me hold a little more tightly onto my father's chest...and the comforting squeeze that lets me know I am safe...the vendors barking out challenges to anyone who will listen...baseballs whapping against a canvas net as burly men heave

Even when it

seems that

your toddler

is not

absorbing

and learning,

you can bet

he is.

them at bowling pins with all their might…a million lights flashing…the thrill and terror of embarking on a ride…the cotton candy lady rapidly stirring her concoction, and the skip of my heart as she hands us a wonderful pink cloud…and how it tickles my nose when I try to take a bite, and melts in my mouth so quickly that it startles me…feeling my heart drop into my stomach as the Ferris wheel whisks us high above the din into the cool night air…looking around at the wonderful view from above…and then my heart dropping again as we plummet earthward once more….

Being a toddler is like that first carnival, a state of perpetual sensory overload. Experiences come rapidly and are absorbed, categorized, analyzed, compared, written into the permanent memory and employed again in the mind of a toddler faster than in any computer known to man. Even when it seems that your toddler is not absorbing and learning, you can bet he is.

It is within this context that we must discuss building communication skills in toddlers. In this chapter, I will present research demonstrating why this age is so crucial for communication development, review the stages of development you can expect your child to pass through, and list several specific activities you can arrange in your home to maximize your child's learning in this important period of life.

WHY IS COMMUNICATION TRAINING VITAL TO TODDLERS?

Child psychologists have now come to recognize that all of the functions of the intellect are defined and matured at a very early age. Children master spoken language between the ages of one and five, and then spend the rest of their lives smoothing it out and adding to the framework that already exists. Some researchers maintain that the critical years for developing communication competence are all prior to age three! The age at which children increase most rapidly in their vocabulary is probably around the age of learning to walk. Apparently, the advent of a new motor skill is a significant plateau in language development as well. Toddlers learn an average of nine words a day.

WHAT ARE THE STAGES OF SPEECH DEVELOPMENT IN TODDLERS?

The toddler period, while a popular notion, is not a very accurate category for scientific study. I define "toddlerhood" as the period between 18 months and three years of age. Researchers actually divide this age into two segments, the *presyntactic* and *syntactic* periods. *Syntax* is "the orderly arrangement of words," so the presyntactic stage means "before the orderly arrangement of words," generally from 12 to 24 months of age. During this period, the main communication of a child is through gestures and crying, relying on the ability of the parents to interpret and understand. However, the normal child begins saying recognizable words between nine and fourteen months. These first words are usually nouns which the child uses to describe objects in the surrounding environment. Nouns such as bottle, milk, ball and dog occur at about 12 months.

As discussed in the last chapter, children are capable of putting together two and three word sentences at about 1-1/2 to 2 years of age. According to Dr. Roger Brown, a researcher who studied the language development of hundreds of children, these early sentences usually lack connecting words (a, the, and), and fit into six categories:

Some researchers maintain that the critical years for developing communication competence are all prior to age three!

You can	Category	Example
expect your	Reference	"See baby."
toddler to	Nonexistence	"Mommy all gone."
experience	Recurrence	"More milk!"
dramatic	Location	"Dog couch."
spurts in	Possession	"Daddy chair."
language use,	Attribution	"Big ball."

but be patient; every child has his own time schedule.

Interestingly, in any given language, word order comes naturally to a child. The ability to put sentences together properly is built into the structure of the brain. According to Dr. Roger Brown, for example, a child will always say "dog couch" to mean that the dog is on the couch, rather than "couch dog."

You can expect your toddler to experience dramatic spurts in language use. He may amaze you with the way he puts words together into sentences. In preparing for this chapter, I asked my own mother about *my* early sentences. She told me that until 20 months of age, I rarely spoke, but just played quietly (those who know me now find this hard to believe). My first sentence, apparently, was, "I wanna pickle." Complete sentences came suddenly—and continued. My second sentence, incidentally, was uttered as our family drove past a local fast food restaurant: "I smell like french fries." These answers proved my wife's longheld belief that I must have been a strange child!

Your toddler will probably have a short attention span, may enjoy playing alone, and seem often restless. On the other hand, according to Alice Chapin in *Building Your Child's Faith*, toddlers also love pictures, being read to, sung to and rocked. Although "teaching" of language is not advised, there are four ways to stimulate language learning in your toddler: emphasize talking, give experiences which stimulate the child, require communication, and last but not least, read aloud!

EMPHASIZE TALKING!

Since children learn to talk by talking, the best stimulation is to have "live" talk directed toward your child. Decades of research show that families in which talk is directed toward the child have more communicative, intelligent children.

Here are four things to keep in mind when talking with your child:

1. **The child need not respond in order to learn new language skills.** He benefits by paying attention to how others communicate well.

2. **Be sensitive when he wants to communicate with you.** Provide pauses in the conversation so he can respond.

3. **Gradually cut down on answering his questions through non-verbal communication.** This includes shrugging your shoulders, raising your eyebrows, or making dramatic facial gestures. Responding with words forces your toddler to pay more attention to your words and to the environment itself rather than your response to it.

Give your child

opportunities to

experience the

world with all

five senses:

touching,

tasting,

smelling,

looking at, and

hearing. Once

the stuff of his

environment

has emotional

content for him,

you can bet

your toddler

will begin

commenting

on it.

4. **Let common sense be your guide.** No matter how hard they study, researchers haven't come up with any techniques better than mother's intuition! Researchers use the term "motherese" to describe the unique communication style that mothers use with their children. When mothers are with their children they emphasize the present, tailor their vocabulary to the level of the child, paraphrase complicated ideas, use simple yet well-formed sentences, deliberately slow their rate of speech, and use lots of repetition.

PROVIDE STIMULATING EXERIENCES

Children initiate communication about things which interest them. The more fascinating the child's environment, the better. Lots of books, pictures, posters, and toys on shelves will visually stimulate your child's young mind. Give your child opportunities to experience the world with all five senses: touching, tasting, smelling, looking at, and hearing. Once the stuff of his environment has emotional content, you can bet your toddler will begin commenting on it. According to Dr. Mabel Rice, these "comments" will generally express desires, commands, requests and threats, all highly emotional. Exclamations such as "da-da!" or "ma-ma!" or "ball!" or "pret[ty]" just burst right out!

Here are three suggestions for providing stimulating experiences for your toddler:

1. **Emphasize nouns.** Dr. Rice points out that children who first develop a large vocabulary of nouns and then later expand the number of verbs have been found to master grammar more easily. Emphasize nouns by commenting on objects which are of immediate interest to the toddler. For example, if the child seems interested in a wooden spoon, give it to him and comment:

"Spoon. That is a spoon. Do you like spoons? Mommy uses spoons to make something for you to eat. Yes, spoon!"

2. **Answer questions.** Toddlers often ask questions (even if the question is "unh?", meaning "what is that?") simply to hear your voice. As much as possible, give satisfactory answers to your toddler's questions. This will encourage him to ask more questions, often a mixed blessing, but one which will dramatically expand his opportunity to learn language.

3. **Make comparisons.** Help your child understand his environment better by having him analyze it. If your toddler "helps" you in the kitchen by getting all of the pots and pans out, have him make comparisons: which one is bigger, which ones are the same color, which one is red, which one is like the one you are using, or which one is heavy? Enlist your toddler's assistance by having him put spoons, knives and forks in their proper place or arranging storage container lids by size. Simple instructions, accompanied by hardy praise, will turn an everyday event into an opportunity to organize your child's mind.

REQUIRE COMMUNICATION

Perhaps the best way to stimulate your toddler's perception of the environment is to require him to *communicate* verbally to get what he wants. Professor Carol Gibb Harding explains that, "As mothers require certain communicative behaviors before they respond, they are not only encouraging those specific behaviors but also 'teaching' the infant that a mutual means of communication exists." Once the child knows how to use words like "drink," family members should be instructed not to respond to the child's pointing grunts until the child attempts to use the words he knows.

"As mothers require certain communicative behaviors before they respond, they are not only encouraging those specific behaviors but also 'teaching' the infant that a mutual means of communication exists."

Professors Ostrosky and Kaiser, in an essay on "Teaching Exceptional Children," suggest several activities which you can use to require communication in your toddler:

1. **Choice making.** Give your toddler a choice between two toys. Say, "Tell me which one you want" or ask him to name each toy. As he begins to verbalize these responses, teach him alternative ways of asking, such as "Yellow truck, please." At the very least, most children can say "please" and something that sounds like "thank you."

2. **Out of reach.** Place your toddler's favorite toys and books just out of reach, so that he must ask for assistance in getting them.

3. **Assistance.** Show your toddler attractive materials which he will need help in opening or operating. Examples: a drinking bottle, a closed box, or a swing.

4. **Silly situations.** Violate your toddler's expectations. At snack time, for instance, put a ball on his plate rather than a cracker. Attempt to put his shoes on your own feet and see if he comments (either verbally or non-verbally). Put a silly picture on the mirror and see if he notices.

5. **Sabotage.** Require communication by not providing all the materials needed to complete a task. For example, provide a coloring book but no crayons (not the other way around unless you want the furniture redecorated!). If your toddler expresses confusion, encourage him to communicate his need.

6. **Inadequate portions.** At meal or snack time, serve an inadequate portion of food, such as a small piece of a cookie rather than the whole thing. If you are blowing

bubbles, blow just one or two and wait for the child to ask for more. If he is playing with blocks, give him just one block at a time until he asks for what he needs.

NOTE: These episodes should be brief, and should conclude well before they become frustrating to the child! The rule of thumb for educators is that children have a one-minute attention span for each year in age. However, communication play greatly lengthens the attention span, so you may find your child willing to cooperate for longer periods of time.

READ! READ! READ!

Reading aloud serves two functions. First, it broadens your toddler's experiences. Second, it begins to construct the bridge to later reading and writing.

Here are three ideas to enhance reading with your toddler:

1. **Nursery rhymes.** According to Emma Grant Meader, one of the first researchers to apply what is known of communication development to child education, children naturally enjoy rhythm and learn speech best when they can learn it rhythmically.

2. **Sing-song.** Pick up on the words your toddler uses and repeat them in a sing-song voice. When you wish to change the activity, add words or change the words you are "sing-songing." Notice how television programs for children often create simple sing-song phrases to encourage children to be kind, or clean the house. Children pick up on this quickly.

3. **Animated reading.** Make the noise or demonstrate the motion of each character; say, for instance, "A

rabbit goes 'hop, hop, hop,'" and bounce your child slightly. Or ask, "Where is the mouse? Can you put your finger on the mouse?" while helping him do so.

PATIENCE MAKES PERFECT

As in every pursuit, patience produces rewards. You may be surprised at how simple communication, simple games and simple praise advance your toddler's communication skill. If progress is slow, keep in mind that children grow internally first before the results show themselves to the world. You *will* see a difference eventually.

As your child grows in age, his communication needs become more complex. The next chapter focuses on children ages three to seven. In order to describe each activity in more detail, I have provided "project pages" which describe the reason behind each project, the instructions, and variations which give you a virtually infinite set of communication-building projects.

CHAPTER FOURTEEN

AGES THREE TO SEVEN

HOW TO CREATE A DESIRE FOR COMMUNICATION

As with infants and toddlers, many things happen between ages three and seven which make it a vital time for developing communication skills. In this chapter you will discover how to use storytelling, drama, games and other communication development tools to give your child a communication "head start." You will learn how to use your child's desire for communication to teach practical skills such as learning your telephone number.

Before we get started, however, a few pages of introduction will help orient you to the stages of communication development through which your child will progress from ages three to seven. First, we'll discuss what sort of communication skills children are developing during this age range, and then we will overview the six skill areas on which the "project pages" in this chapter will focus.

Incidentally, because of the trial and error nature of communication building in young children, it may be counterproductive to "drill" children in new communication skills. By age eight, children should be ready for the "speech-making" part of communication development. During the three-to-seven years, focus on creating an environment in which your child can explore and direct at least

Focus on creating an environment in which your child can explore and direct at least some of his education himself.

Upgrading the

quality of your

child's play

means

providing the

opportunity for

make-believe

and exploration.

some of his education himself. Imagination, enjoyment and flexibility are the guiding words. If your child begins to think of communication as fun, the foundation you are laying will be that much easier to build on.

How to Use Play to Develop Communication Skills

The most important thing you can do for your child is upgrade his quality of play. Most of his play should be interacting with books, props, self-created toys, and communicating with you and others. It is far better for the child to play "grocery store" or "house" than to watch television or play video games. According to Professors Huckleberry and Strother, constructive, interactive activities allow the child to relive his observations and create vivid impressions about the world.

As a teenager, my parents let me buy a 35-year-old pickup truck at an auction. My youngest brother and sister got as much use out of the truck as I did. Parked in the back yard, they loved using it as a springboard to imaginative adventures: one day it would be a fire truck (complete with garden hoses), the next a farm truck, (with our two dogs playing their assigned roles as cows or sheep), or whatever. No toy could have provided such creative play opportunities, and both children grew into creative and talented young people.

Upgrading the quality of your child's play means providing the opportunity for make-believe and exploration. Yet keep in mind that creativity does not occur in a vacuum: a musician must master the fundamentals of music in order to exercise "creativity." As professors Huckleberry and Strother remind us, "Creativity needs social judgement so that it may be examined and refined."

COMMUNICATION DEVELOPMENT BETWEEN AGES THREE AND SEVEN

We'll discuss what sort of fundamentals you can work on with your child in just a minute. First, let's take a bird's eye view of the sort of changes you'll notice in your increasingly communicative child.

BECOMING MORE ARTICULATE

By age five, children should have fully intelligible speech, although some lack of articulation is normal. Children this age will use complex sentences and clauses. If your child is having a problem with these, arrange a checkup with a speech therapist.

Starting toward the beginning of this age range, your child should gradually be weaned from gesture language. Experts believe that gradually refusing to understand and respond to the child's tendency to "point and grunt" is a major step in bringing about true speech. Experiment: Use pantomime and gesture to draw communication out of your child. Say, "Now *you* try to guess what I am pointing to." Grunt a few times until he becomes frustrated with his inability to decipher your communication. It won't be long before these teachable moments move your child in the direction of clearer communication.

In addition, begin expanding your use of conversation with your child. Drs. Dance and Larson have theorized that talk which helps your child "displace" from the immediate situation is very helpful in expanding the usefulness of language for him. This means asking your child questions about the past ("Do you remember where we went in the car yesterday?") or the future ("What do you think we will see when we go to the zoo tomorrow?").

Although it will be difficult, experts believe that gradually refusing to understand and respond to the child's tendency to "point and grunt" is a major step in bringing about true speech.

Keep in mind

that during the

three-to-seven

stage, children

understand far

more words

than they

actually use.

DEVELOPING A LARGER VOCABULARY

Children develop so rapidly from three to seven that at first glance; it seems futile to even highlight such a range for this book. However, while development is rapid, it is more an expansion of existing skills rather than development of new ones. Vocabulary, for example, will grow rapidly, usually tripling between the second and third year, and doubling again by age five with as many as 1,800 words in correct use. Your child might even make up some words of his own. One of our family favorites is "Sprickles," which are the rays of the sun. Enjoy this time of creativity!

Also by age three children begin to correctly use pronouns, make comparisons (big vs. little), and recognize and point out colors. "Baby talk" should begin to diminish, as you stop using it and gradually and gently quit reinforcing it in your child.

You can enhance your child's vocabulary development by playing naming games. Ask questions such as, "Can you see three things that are white?" and "Whar can you see out the window?" Show your child a picture of an object such as a car, and ask, "What are all the words you can think of to describe that car?" Simple questions such as these will help your child learn to recall and use words he knows, an important vocabulary building activity.

Keep in mind that during the three-to-seven stage, children understand far more words than they actually use. By age six, for example, your child may have an expressive vocabulary of about 2,500 words, but understand up to 15,000 words. The wider the range of experiences your child has, the higher this so-called "receptive" vocabulary will be.

DEVELOPING A BETTER UNDERSTANDING OF EMOTIONS

As they emerge from the toddler stage, children deepen in their recognition of emotions in others. Professor Baltaxe reviewed studies showing that at age five, boys perceive emotions more accurately than girls, but these results are reversed in children ages six to twelve. Children who have weathered emotional trauma during the toddler stage may experience more difficulty in recognizing emotion in the voice and facial expressions of adults. All of this means that your child will be sensitive to your moods, and may actually react to them. This is all a natural part of learning to communicate with others.

Here is a simple way to reinforce your child's recognition of emotions: using cheap paper plates, draw eyes and a mouth to reflect different emotions. Here are five examples:

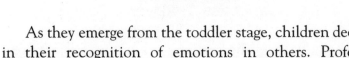

To create other variations, use pieces of yarn to create different eye and mouth shapes. Mimic what your child creates and have him mimic what you create. Your child will immediately begin to observe the facial expressions of others and even think more carefully about his own expressions. A good spiritual lesson here, incidentally, is to teach your child what sort of expressions indicate that someone is angry. Read the Proverbs that tell us about angry people, such as, "An angry man stirs up dissension, and a hot-tempered one commits many sins" Proverbs 29:22 (NIV).

Mimic what your child creates and have him mimic what you create. Your child will immediately begin to observe the facial expressions of others and even think more carefully about his own expressions.

SIX AREAS OF VITAL
COMMUNICATION DEVELOPMENT
BETWEEN AGES THREE AND SEVEN

The projects in this section work on six different areas of communication development in a fun and creative way. Whether you use them in an educational or recreational fashion, being aware of the six specific skills will allow you as a parent to sense the areas of greatest importance for your child.

1. **Smoothness.** Elise Hahn's classic study of six-year-olds demonstrated that at least 50 percent of children need to overcome broken or choppy rhythm, and more than one out of three demonstrate a very narrow range of inflection. One out of four speak too softly, and over a third fail to articulate and pronounce words properly. Working on these skills might involve:

   • **Rhythm.** Assist your child in overcoming false starts, repetition of words and phrases, and purposeless hesitations.

   Idea: "Let's pretend the world is in slow motion, so we must talk more slowly."

   Point: "Sometimes our mouths get ahead of our brains!"

   • **Volume.** Demonstrate and practice soft or loud volume as the particular occasion demands.

   Idea: "Let's practice soft and loud voices. Why don't you say your Bible verse very, very softly, and then move farther away and get louder, and then close again."

Point: "We must be careful to use the right loudness depending on how close or far away we are." When answering the telephone, for example, don't yell for the requested person into the ear of the caller!

- **Pitch.** Engage in activities which broaden your child's range of inflection while teaching him to control emotion in his voice.

Idea: "Let's practice what different animals might sound like if they could talk: high, low, soft, and loud. What would a robot sound like?" You can even have singsongy repetitions, such as a beginning children's piano lesson I once heard:

"Hel $_{lo}$ Bar ^{ney} my ^{y} name's ———."

This teaches voice inflection, reinforced by high and low keys on the piano.

Point: "If we want others to listen, we must not talk like robots. We must use our voices in an interesting way."

- **Timing.** Work to smooth awkward hesitations, breathlessness, and slowness.

Idea: (Getting down on the child's eye level) "Don't worry, I'm listening! I would like for you to slow down, collect your thoughts, and then tell me what you need to say."

Point: "People sometimes lose track of what you are saying, so be careful to speak smoothly without stopping a lot."

Keep these points in mind as you work through the activities in this section.

2. **Discernment.** Learn color, shapes, size, rhythm, good vs. evil, and loud vs. soft. You can enhance your child's motor skills through marching, clapping, tapping, judging space, size, color, and judging of emotional states.

- **Colors.** Announce a special day to celebrate a particular color. On "Green Day" have your child wear green clothes, look for green in the great outdoors, put lettuce on his sandwich, and use food coloring to make green frosting for his graham crackers. Play a game, "I see green." Give hints to your child until he guesses what you are seeing.

- **Shapes.** Announce a "round day," for instance. Cut sandwiches into circles, make round cookies, and look for round things in the neighborhood.

  Think of other activities which reinforce the discernment between various things. Discernment is the key to observation, which is the foundation of many of the most significant communication skills.

3. **Clarity.** Speech is not truly communication until others understand what the child is trying to say. For example, say, "I am trying to understand what you are saying. Help me. Say it again for me. Again, slowly. Point to something to help me understand you." With patience, you will develop a system of reinforcement that also builds your relationship. Once again, use gentle coaching rather than "drills."

4. **Appropriate language.** Appropriate language focuses on the effectiveness of communication in various speaking situations. Children between ages three and seven are old enough to begin learning how to communicate in a socially acceptable way. Most people believe that it is improper etiquette for a young child

to treat adults like children, or to communicate a lack of respect for authority. Practicing appropriate language helps children understand what constitutes proper behavior in social situations. Social graces, much like those taught by Professor Higgins to Eliza in "My Fair Lady," are learned through practice and repetition. Teach each skill to your child, reinforce it, praise him for his improvement, and practice it again.

5. **Quick, effective thinking.** Children can enjoy learning to think quickly, connecting names with objects, comparing one thing to another, processing information out loud without boring the listener, and becoming more observant.

6. **Courteous and critical listening.** Children will practice hearing, understanding, remembering, discerning and judging as they learn to interact more effectively with the world around them. As a child, I balked at attending family reunions. "It's just a bunch of old people," I complained. Then my mother arranged for "story circles," in which family members sat and visited about their childhood experiences. Fascinated and impressed, I saw these elderly relatives in a new light, interacting with them differently from that point forward.

HOW TO USE THE "PROJECT PAGES"

Now that we have discussed the six skill areas on which the projects in this chapter will focus, you are ready to begin. I suggest first skimming all of the projects to get an idea of an order in which you would like to try them. Also, keep in mind that simple completion of a project does not guarantee mastery of it. Rather, each project should be used repeatedly, as opportunities arise, to create a wealth of communication *experiences* for your child.

NOTES

STORYTELLING

Project Sketch

Storytelling is perhaps the best way to invigorate communication skills in small children. Stories infused with emotion will enhance both their memory and imagination. When children listen to a well-told story and repeat it, they are able to develop strong memories and use them imaginatively. As Mary Jo Puckett-Cliatt and Jean Shaw explain, as children retell the story, they move from being passive listeners to active participants in the story-making process. This storytelling project is followed by several related projects, giving you a wealth of ideas for this important approach to communication development!

How-To

Simply create a story from scratch or relate one from a children's book. Tell the story slowly, using facial expression and voice inflection. Take on the role of the characters, using their "voices" and emotions. You might even make the story memorable through costumes or sound effects.

When you finish, ask your child questions about it. He should be able to remember the central point, characters' names, the pictures, the emotional state of the characters, choose which of the events happened first, etc. You can also ask about what the story means, what the author wanted him to learn, and how he might respond if he were in a similar situation.

Ask your child to retell the story as best as he can remember. Encourage him with warm, positive feedback, such as "Yes! *Then* what happened?" Clap when he finishes. The purpose of this activity is to capture the essential components and the emotion with which the story can be told. Over time, require greater detail, such as correct order of events and dialogue. Encourage your child to tell the story to friends and relatives for additional reinforcement.

Elements to focus on: conveying the story with clarity (so that other adults could understand), placing the elements of the story in the correct order, using different voices to represent different characters and their emotional states, and gesturing. As you repeat this activity on a regular basis, your child should be able to listen for the central point, recognize what kind of voice is needed to convey emotion and characterization, and develop smoother mannerisms, a sense of rhythm, and the ability to invent dialogue.

TIMELY TIP

Children especially like stories which incorporate *them* as characters or which tell of your own childhood. My mother, for instance, enrolled in a writing class and was assigned the task of recalling and recording childhood stories. These stories became the joy of the whole family!

FUTURE ADVENTURE

Create check points in stories. Stop at crucial points and ask the child what happens next or what should happen next, "sabotage" the story by using voices which don't match the characters (such as a high, squeaky voice for the giant) and get your child to "correct you."

MAKE IT MEMORABLE!

If you have a piano, allow your child to compose an accompaniment while you read, or allow him to use pots and pans and other household items to reinforce the rhythmical, musical nature of stories. Sound effects are simple to create; tapping shoes on a large piece of cardboard with sand on top gives the effect of footsteps. Banging two dried coconut halves together simulates the sound of horses' hooves. Crinkling tin foil sounds like firecrackers. Use your imagination!

NOTES

MAGNETIC STORIES

PROJECT SKETCH

This activity allows you to focus on placing characters in the past and present, developing a theme, and teaching your child to recognize and repeat a sequence of events in the proper order. It also gives your child "props" to ease his transition into storytelling.

HOW-TO

Cut out pictures from magazines, paste them onto a poster board or "chip" board backing, and cut to size. Magnetic strips with adhesive backing are available from most discount stores. Place the magnets on the backs of the pictures, and ask your child to create a story by arranging pictures in sequence on a cookie sheet.

TIMELY TIP

If your child needs encouragement, begin by telling a story yourself, asking him to place the cut-outs on a cookie sheet for you. When finished, take the pictures down and ask the child to verbally reconstruct the story as he places them back on the cookie sheet.

FUTURE ADVENTURE

Flannel Graph Stories. Create a story board approximately 3' by 3' from reinforced cardboard and cover with flannel material purchased at a discount store. Bible story characters and many other items may be purchased from any large Christian educational supplier. Cut out the characters and place them on the board as the story progresses. Flannel graph stories provide a visually exciting story option.

MAKE IT MEMORABLE!

The refrigerator is often a central message center in a home. Stick magnetic cut-outs on the refrigerator so your child can make up stories or practice old ones while you are busy in the kitchen.

SEQUENCE STORIES

PROJECT SKETCH

Stories enhance thinking skills largely by teaching that what happens later in the story is affected by what happens first. Actions have consequences, and decisions made by characters will influence the outcome of the story. Learning to think sequentially is a valuable lesson in life as well as an important exercise in developing logical thinking and speaking skills.

HOW-TO

Clothesline stories. To focus on the sequence of events in a story, tie a clothesline in the room and have your child clip pictures to it based on the action found in the story. After you tell your sequential story several times, let your child try it.

Map stories. To help your child focus on the sequence of events, as well as to teach map skills and perspective, draw a large map of the area where your story might take place. For example, draw a map of the battlefield where David met Goliath. Along the path, glue "pop-ups" of the characters or scenery one might encounter. Place pop-ups face down so your child can stand them up as the story progresses.

TIMELY TIP

You may need to explain what a map is and why we use them. Once your child grasps the concept, encourage him to put events that occur in the story in the correct order. Focus on the "gist" of the story, not the details.

FUTURE ADVENTURE

Use map stories to follow up your child's experiences with the popular media. After viewing a movie, have him draw a map of where the action might have taken place and create characters. This reinforces the idea of sequence in the "real world" and allows a simple learning tool to enhance outside entertainment.

MAKE IT MEMORABLE!

Tie stories into real life! Use real maps and a globe to help your child gain a sense of place (i.e., where he lives, where the story takes place or where the author lived). If the story takes place in another country, try to convey how far away it is and how the culture might have influenced the author to write as he did.

CARTOON STORIES

PROJECT SKETCH

Much of effective communication involves organizing one's thoughts and relaying information in a sequential manner. The purpose of this activity is to create an awareness of how a plot unfolds and creates action in a story.

HOW-TO

Show your child several cartoon strips from the newspaper, reading the words and explaining the action. Then work with your child to create your own cartoons! Begin by drawing pictures detailing a sequence of actions. This might include: the number of objects in the picture increasing, the size of something expanding (as someone inflates a balloon), or someone with food on the plate, eating and then having eaten something. Ask your child to describe the action involved, and speculate on what the characters might say. As he begins to grasp the idea that things happen in a time-space sequence, you can encourage your child to actually tell the story represented by the cartoon. This activity may be repeated over and over again, even spontaneously in the car or while waiting at the doctor's office.

TIMELY TIP

Do not worry if your drawings seem elementary. Unless you're headed for syndication, just focus on making sure the content is sequential! Also, encourage your child to sign his name in the corner and date each cartoon, placing them in a scrapbook. He will enjoy looking at them over and over.

FUTURE ADVENTURE

Using liquid correction fluid, white out the words in newspaper cartoons and ask your child to come up with his own. Paste them into a notebook to keep. You can even make several pages of cartoons at once to keep your child occupied in a creative activity.

MAKE IT MEMORABLE!

Allow your child to create his own cartoons. With a ruler, draw a sequence of 12 boxes (four each in three lines) on a sheet of white paper, and make several photocopies (make the boxes larger for younger children). Draw pictures inside these boxes. Once the pictures are drawn, try to guess what is happening, or have the child describe the situation. Record the dialogue in the space below the picture. Explain to your child the idea of "blocking," that television advertisements, cartoons and movies are made by first drawing a one-frame picture of each scene. You can use these sheets for "blocking" later puppet shows and drama productions. Who knows! You may have a budding screenwriter in the family!

SITUATION CARDS

PROJECT SKETCH

The purpose of this activity is to create "ready-made" dramatic situations from which your child can create a story. This allows him to become creative with what he is given, merging it with his own efforts. It will also give your child the opportunity to think about interesting character traits: what makes a person good or bad, and how to change one's own life to have stronger character.

HOW-TO

Write down several simple descriptions of situations or objects and put them in a box. You can also have your child contribute situations. Examples of situations include:

1. *You walk out into the back yard and discover an old shed with a rusty lock.*

2. *You wake up in the morning and find that instead of being in your bed, you are in a cave, and a friendly dinosaur is sniffing at you.*

3. *You are in the Old West riding on a wagon train.*

4. *You suddenly wake up and find yourself in a beautiful castle. A servant comes in and asks "What would you like to do today, O' Queen? (or King)?"*

5. *You hear a knock on the door. When you open it, there is a box with a small puppy in it.*

Ask the child to draw from the box and create a story based on the situation.

An off-shoot of this project is to have your child choose from among three or four sacks, closed, with objects inside. Upon opening the sack, they can make up a story about the item inside. Your child can make whole stories out of items such as a tea bag, a treasure map, a pneumatic drill, an unusual flower, or bubble gum! For variations, allow your child to draw a card from which *you* make up a story. Incorporate elements of effective communication and set a good example!

TIMELY TIP

If your child has difficulty, ask questions which draw out his own creativity, such as "what do you suppose would be inside the shed?", "What kind of things are usually inside a shed?", "What would surprise you if you found it in there?" Questions are better than actual suggestions. In addition, save the cards, since there is an infinite number of stories which may be created from each!

FUTURE ADVENTURES

1. **Make several boxes:** one for characters (including animals) and one for situations in which characters might find themselves. For older children, include one for items to include in the story, one for the physical descriptions of characters, and even one for moods. Each story should include one situation, at least two characters with physical descriptions and moods, and three items which must be included in the story.

2. **Use an old apron with pockets instead of boxes.** The storyteller, whether adult or child, gets to wear the apron and draw cards out of the pockets. You can even cut out pictures, paste them on cardboard, and fasten them to the apron as the story progresses.

3. **Fish for a story.** Decorate a large cardboard box with an ocean theme. Paste magnet strips (available at all discount stores) to the back of magazine cutouts mounted on cardboard. Make a fishing rod with a dowel and string, with another magnet on the end of the string. The child fishes out elements and tells a story about each.

MAKE IT MEMORABLE

Allow your child to decorate the storyteller's box with tin foil, construction paper, and cut-outs. Make it special!

NOTES

HALF-TOLD STORY

PROJECT SKETCH

Another way to make storytelling interesting and exciting to your child is the half-told story. The half-told story will teach your child to listen carefully to the details of the story, and then insert himself into the plot and answer the "what-if" questions that arise. Most important, this storytelling technique will teach your child how to resolve a plot and create a definite ending to a story. He will learn to initiate and complete thoughts in a precise, imaginative manner.

HOW-TO

There are two ways to create the story. First, create it as you go, with you and your child taking turns adding lines. Here's a sample:

Adult: *Johnnie Jensen went into the garage and got his fishing pole and a shovel.*

Child: *Then he dug some big fat worms from the garden and went fishing.*

Adult: *Well, he started to go fishing, but first he decided he would like a friend to go with him, so…*

Child: *He asked Allen to go with him.*

Adult: *Allen said, "I cannot go because I have to stay home to practice my piano." So Johnnie thought, "What shall I do?" He went to Brad's house and knocked and knocked on the door.*

Notice how the adult keeps the story going and adds complex processes, action, sound effects, characters and dialogue.

The second way to develop a story is to share the first half of a new story with your child, leaving off at a crucial point in the action: a dangerous predicament, a difficult decision, or a moral dilemma. Leave enough cues to ensure a development of action.

When the child finishes, compare your ending with his. Ask questions which encourage him to discern the dilemmas which arise about good vs. evil, and what good and bad characters act like.

Focus on helping your child create dialogue, remembering enough details from your half of the story to incorporate them into his half. If your child starts to stray from the descriptions of characters as given, or inadvertently changes or forgets something, ask questions to lead him back to it. The purpose is to construct a faithful ending to an already existing story.

Use an old three-ring binder or portfolio to hold the half-created stories, both yours and your child's. Allow your child to decorate the binder with magic markers. If you wish, use paper report folders or snap-lock binders, one for each story. Leave enough room on each page for drawings which accompany the story line. Have the child "read" or tell the story to younger siblings, neighborhood children, relatives or guests in your home. His pride in his work will make it easier for him to communicate with others, which is, of course, the whole point of this project!

TIMELY TIP

Encourage creativity and vivid detail. Instead of simply a "giant," the child could tell of an "enormous, loud man, eighteen feet high with size 96 shoes and beady eyes, who hadn't shaved in probably forty-two years."

Future Adventures

1. Have your child construct the story, and *you* finish it.

2. Have your child take on the persona of one of the characters and finish the story from their perspective.

3. Tell the story to a tape recorder for later editing and transfer to paper.

Make It Memorable

Write down each ending created and "publish" it as a completed story, with you and your child as the authors! Nice binders with occasional color pictures make your child's investment of time seem more worthwhile.

NOTES

STORY-ROUND-THE-FAMILY

Project Sketch

The purpose of this activity is to enhance your child's ability to think quickly and imaginatively. It is also great for family time, being particularly suitable for car trips, dinner-time conversation, or time around the campfire. It teaches your child how to create and build suspense. Because suspense creates curiosity in the audience, it is one of the communicator's most useful tools.

How-To

Begin a story which you tell for a minute or so and then leave at a point of interest. Each participant continues the story and also leaves it at a point of interest. This technique may be used with as many as six people without losing its focus, or it can be traded back and forth between adult and child.

Each story should contain an economy of incidents, usually three. You can control this by thinking of three objects that should play into the story: a bear, an old red flannel shirt, and a blender, for example. The more unexpected, the better. Of course, both children and adults will require a great deal of practice! Once you try it just a few times, you will find it easy to create an interesting, creative story.

Again, create as many details as possible: years, background situations, specific amounts, and specific times. Make the characters interesting as well. Reward specific descriptions with praise: "Wow, that is really specific!" or "I can almost see the giant as you describe him!" or "That's a very creative way to describe someone." If details are hard to elicit, ask questions which lead your child in that direction: "What do you suppose the giant would look like? Hairy or bald? Skinny or fat? *How* skinny or fat? So skinny that when he turns sideways, he nearly disappears? So fat that it takes 16 minutes for the grease from his fried chicken to dribble all the way down his 16 chins?"

TIMELY TIPS

1. **Work in a lesson on character.** Debrief stories by asking "what if" questions, determining whether the characters were heroes or villains and what made them that way.

2. **Play an adjective game.** If your child is finding it difficult to describe a character or situation in detail, stop the story and have the entire family brainstorm about possible descriptions.

FUTURE ADVENTURE

Give your child the opportunity to pick an incident, item, character, or setting for the story.

PUPPETS

PROJECT SKETCH

A puppet show can either be a planned or spontaneous activity, and can be accomplished even by children who are pre-verbal. There are many benefits to using puppets to build communication skills: 1) they demonstrate the connection between body movements, emotional expression, and words, 2) they provide an example of a story line and plot progression, and 3) they give an opportunity to perform without the pressure of standing in front of an audience.

HOW-TO

Make a puppet stage by simply spreading a sheet over two chairs. A custom stage may be made with a cardboard "cutting board" used for sewing. Find one that folds up in an accordion fashion, and cover it with wrapping paper. You could also use shipping boxes from appliances or home office equipment, cutting them to size. Adding windows or special features makes a puppet stage even more fun.

Puppets can be made from paper dolls or flannel graph figures glued to old socks. Or you could decorate socks with magic markers and cloth scraps cut into costumes and facial features. If your budget allows, purchase some t-shirt paint from a craft store and paint white socks with it. Children especially enjoy paint which puffs when ironed. Be creative! Any old household items can serve as puppets or props.

Use puppets to: 1) carry out any storytelling activity, 2) demonstrate a concept or task, 3) occupy your child as you or one of your older children tell a story, 4) help your child act out a story as you read it, and 5) allow your child to create a puppet play based on a story he has written.

Encourage experimentation! Your child may want to play with the stage, create his own puppet characters and conduct plays on his own time. This is the kind of play that builds communication skills!

TIMELY TIPS

1. **Have your child watch as well as perform, so he can see what his puppet movements might look like.** Videotape him for playback if you have equipment available.

2. **Use puppets to help your child refine his perception of emotions.** While you work the puppet, have him guess which emotion is being expressed: happiness (whistling), anger (yelling), sadness (crying or moaning), surprise (wide open mouth with a quick air intake), etc. Exaggerate at first, and become more subtle as the child grows older.

FUTURE ADVENTURES

1. **Bible stories.** Alice Chapin suggests that you can use drama to reinforce scripture lessons by making puppets represent biblical characters, and using the stage to act out stories as you read. For example, an animal puppet could tell an animal story (Noah's ark, Balaam's donkey, or Daniel in the lions' den).

2. **Life-size cutouts.** As an interesting alternative to puppets, use large pieces of cardboard to make "life-size" cutouts of the characters in the story.

MAKE IT MEMORABLE!

You can help your child improve communicatively by getting him to interact with puppets. Encourage your child to ask questions of the puppet, such as "What is your job?" or "What makes you happy or sad?" A friendly puppet can help small children overcome shyness. If your child doesn't speak loudly enough for others to hear, a "hard of hearing" puppet can prompt him to speak loudly and slowly. Or if your child is restricted in using gestures, this same puppet may "benefit" from having things acted out in pantomime.

One last hint: keep the puppets special by boxing them up as you would a game, rather than throwing them in a toy box. Also, try to "keep them" from biting the fingers of the audience and other such playing. Puppets will be more useful for story-telling and related play if they maintain a higher status than mere toys.

NOTES

DRAMA

PROJECT SKETCH

The ability to demonstrate dramatic behavior (as opposed to melodramatic behavior) will greatly enhance your child's ability to express himself effectively. Drama helps children develop clear, audible speech while allowing them to express personality, a sense of humor, and flexibility. Drama draws from and reinforces drawing, writing and storytelling skills, since children often use body language and oral language to communicate meaning.

HOW-TO

Use your imagination and encourage your child to use his in creating props and dramatic circumstances. The goal of the present activity is *expressiveness*. Professors Huckleberry and Strother suggest you begin with simple exercises such as, "Show me how a lazy man walks," "Show me how a burglar walks," or "Show me how a little girl chases a butterfly." Or you can ask questions about stories you have read together: for example, "What does Snow White say and do when she wakes from her long sleep?" Be sure to applaud and teach your child to say "thank you" by bowing.

Another simple way to start is for your child to act out stories as you read to him. During Christmas time, he can act out Mary and Joseph journeying to Bethlehem. Reinforce his acting with questions: What does the donkey do? How does it eat and drink? What do the angels and shepherds do? Each activity should reinforce drama skills, getting your child to use his body to be expressive.

TIMELY TIP

1. **Focus on dialogue.** One of the benefits of a dramatic activity is that it can reinforce the role of dialogue in increasing excitement.

2. **Use the situation cards discussed in this chapter.** This is especially fun if there is more than one child, because they can play off of each other in impromptu acting. One example suggested by Diana Morgan is two children sit on a bench, one feels for his watch and it is gone, so he accuses the other of taking it, etc.

3. **Define your expectations.** Decide how much educational value you want the activity to include. Children enjoy creating their own dramas, but also need to be challenged to add structure, plot and well-developed characters to their efforts.

4. **Encourage creative set design.** There is an important, yet somewhat intangible benefit for children learning how to use lighting, design costumes, and create props. You can probably find a wealth of creative and hilarious props at second-hand stores and garage sales.

FUTURE ADVENTURES

1. **Reinforce the reading skills of your older children by asking them to read while the younger children act.** Make fun "rules" for this time, such as the more vividly the story is read, the more dramatic the action must be.

2. **Play charades.** Silent acting forces dramatic behavior, since the child cannot use his voice to emphasize his acting.

MAKE IT MEMORABLE!

Gather an audience. Just like adults, children need to learn to derive satisfaction from an activity planned and executed. Allow your child to "sell" tickets to family members for the performance. As he gets better, maybe he could conduct a neighborhood "drama club" during the summer!

NOTES

RECITATION

PROJECT SKETCH

In ancient Hebrew culture children began memorization at a very early age. Bible passages which formed acrostics helped Hebrew children memorize the alphabet. Proverbs and sayings committed to memory using rhyming poetic forms helped children remember important information. Psalms set to music and dancing sealed biblical principles into the mind. Even today, difficult information memorized in a rhyming form or using mnemonic techniques is much easier to recall than mere lists. Memorizing and reciting short Bible verses and poems are an exciting way for young children to begin working on verbal skills. Poems and rhyming verse, especially when accompanied by physical activity, may actually strengthen the cognitive foundation for future learning.

HOW-TO

Children as young as 20 months can "fill in the blanks" in a simple story that you recite. Four-and five-year-olds love memorizing simple poems and rhymes. Finding good materials may be your most difficult task. First, check your local library for books with nursery rhymes and poems for children. You may opt to purchase some books at a Christian bookstore. Used bookstores often offer a large children's section.

Poems may be memorized while riding in the car or just lying down looking at the sky. I still remember a poem I learned in kindergarten:

If I had a spoon as tall as the sky,
    I'd dish up some clouds as they go slip-sliding by
I'd take them inside and give them a cook
    and see if they taste as good as they look.

TIMELY TIPS

As Professors Huckleberry and Strother indicate, young children enjoy the "short and sweetness" of poems, so don't try to introduce difficult concepts yet. Select poems that might be accompanied by physical activity such as jumping, skipping or dancing ("I'm a little teapot" is a good example). For young children, exercising motor skills helps both memorization and oral delivery.

FUTURE ADVENTURE

"Fill-in-the-blank" stories. Obviously, a child who can barely speak will face some limitations at memorizing poems and scripture verses. But as soon as he masters a few words, you can teach him fill-in-the-blank stories. I recently observed a mother and 20-month-old child who had studied the story of Jonah. It went something like this: "Jonah was a man who *disobeyed* God. He *ran (making running motions)* away and got on a *boat*. The waves came up *(wavy motions with arms)* and the men threw Jonah into the water *(splashing sound)*. A big *fish* came and swallowed Jonah *(gulping sound)*. Then Jonah prayed *(with praying motions)* and the fish *spit (with spitting sound)* Jonah onto the *beach*. After that, Jonah *obeyed*."

MAKE IT MEMORABLE!

Memorize Bible verses. Young children can understand the basic truths found in Scripture. Even very young children can memorize Bible verses that are paraphrased simply, such as in the Living Bible. At a Christian book store, ask for a Bible memory program for children which allows them to memorize a verse for each letter of the alphabet, and contains a poem accompanying each verse. Otherwise, select a verse for your child and develop your own program. Your child can transfer the verse and poems to a scrapbook which he decorates with crayons, markers, or glitter glue.

DRAWING

PROJECT SKETCH

According to Lee Karnowski in an essay on how young writers communicate, speech can be a pre-writing strategy when it is used to explore a topic and decide on the content of a story or discourse. While adults communicate primarily through words, and resort to graphs and pictures for further explanation, children use art, music and drama to make sense of the writing process. For younger children who do not yet know how to "write," try drawing. Your child can draw a picture and communicate the story behind it, or simply describe what he has drawn. Many children will communicate orally as they draw, or they may hum or sing. While this activity may seem simple, it is also profoundly meaningful. It allows the child to focus on oral communication skills as a part of everyday life.

HOW-TO

Give your child drawing material and ask him to make a picture. Encourage him to tell you out loud what he is going to draw and ask questions as he does it. When he finishes, sit with him and listen to the story behind the picture. if he simply describes its elements, encourage him to make up a story to go with it.

TIMELY TIP

Remember that the purpose of this activity is oral communication, which means that you should be present! Some families have created a play room or craft room with the noble intention of hiding their child's sometimes messy activities. However, your adult presence and oral interaction will make a qualitative difference in everyday play.

FUTURE ADVENTURES

1. **Play a music tape while the child draws.** Music soothes the soul and enhances creativity. According to Mr. Karnowski, children actually use the sounds of music to make meaning. You can also play a story tape and ask your child to draw the action and characters, or simply whatever comes to mind.

2. **Use crafts other than drawing.** Walk through a large craft store sometime just to see what is available: they have everything from colored glue to plastic beads which melt together to form colorful place mats. Money invested in craft materials is almost always a wiser investment than the toys advertised on Saturday morning television!

MAKE IT MEMORABLE!

Encourage drawing or coloring when you read together as a family. Every member of the family will enjoy drawing, coloring, stitching or assembling models while listening. On an 11" by 17" piece of paper, use a black magic marker to draw an outline of a picture and a short saying or scripture that reinforces the lesson. Make photocopies for the family, and allow them to color as you read. Occasionally, take these masterpieces back to the copy store and have them laminated. My parents have a whole drawer of such "place mats" in which their children took great pride!

JOURNALING

PROJECT SKETCH

Journaling provides an excellent opportunity to refine and communicate thoughts and feelings. It also helps the child learn to reflect on his experiences and to begin focusing on the world outside. A journal might include commentary on a family vacation or field trip, letters to oneself, observations of the world, and reflections on pleasures and disappointments.

HOW-TO

Children ages three to seven are almost exclusively in a pre-writing stage. This means that any journaling must be dictated to you. Just as you help him write down stories and "publish" them, help your child record his thoughts, feelings and perceptions.

TIMELY TIPS

1. **If you are writing the journal on behalf of your child, resist the temptation to "fill in" details which the child does not give.** Writing down his observations as closely as you can to what he offers will provide a means of evaluating his improvement over a period of time.

2. **Ask questions instead of making suggestions.** The journal should be the child's creation, and he may have a clear preference for what sorts of things he would like to have in it. If he is stumped or seems at a loss for words, ask questions which draw out his thoughts.

FUTURE ADVENTURES

1. **Note-taking.** Take time on a trip or outing to help your child record his observations. Note-taking can be as simple as writing down what colors he sees, how many trucks, windmills, and barns. It can also include sense-impressions: What do you see? How does it make you feel? What do you expect to see when we get there? How do the buildings, homes and people look different here than at home? What smells are here? Have you heard any new sounds?

2. **Have the child help with writing.** If you are writing letters to relatives or friends, ask your child to dictate to you some things he would like to tell that person. If old enough to write, he can do it himself. If not, maybe he can sign his name or draw a simple picture. Either way, it gets him to see firsthand the value of communication!

MAKE IT MEMORABLE!

Make lists. Children like to make lists. Encourage this! Your child can use lists to become more organized, understand the sequence of events for the day, or make a list of tasks to be accomplished. For younger children, lists may be as simple as recording desired Christmas or birthday gifts or listing toys in a certain order (by group, kind, preference, etc.).

Take pictures. Photograph events and order double copies. Give one set to your child to paste in his own scrapbook. As he tells the "cut line" that goes with each picture, write it underneath. Include the dates and names of the people and places in the pictures. Encourage your child to share his scrapbook with guests in your home, or to take it along when you go visiting.

COPYING

PROJECT SKETCH

Speech, as in all child behaviors, emerges in part through children copying adult behavior. Therefore, the more opportunities a child has to copy, and in the greater number of contexts, the deeper the learning experience. Copying enhances a child's powers of observation, a foundational ability which feeds into communication skill.

HOW-TO

Show your child how to copy pictures, and encourage him to copy anything he finds interesting: the words to an appealing song, poems, Bible verses or quotations from books. Allow him to decorate and post them on the wall. If your child is unable to write, suggest that he allow you to help him.

TIMELY TIP

Once again, involvement is more important than perfection. The complexity of that which is being copied and the art involved should match the child's skill level. Don't be concerned if the copied version bears no resemblance to the original! At this point in life, the child's perceptions of objects or situations may be far different from your own, and his motor skills are not as refined as yours. Resist the temptation to get him drawing "within the lines" at too early an age.

FUTURE ADVENTURE

Give your child poems, quotations and Bible verses of enduring value to copy. Those which promote positive character traits will have timeless value in the life of the child. In church, children can benefit from copying hymn titles and page numbers and still manage to catch some of the sermon!

MAKE IT MEMORABLE

Encourage your child to copy *occasions* as well as objects. Your child might "preach" behind a pulpit, design a "movie set," host a "talk show," or produce his own radio and television advertisements. [Note: this is one occasion in which the child's imagination might be exercised more if you are *not* there to observe. Let him take chances by himself first. He will let you know when he is ready to perform!] A piano bench with a tinker toy microphone makes a wonderful pulpit from which to preach. A card table can serve as the desk for a talk show host. A movie camera can be crafted from an empty cereal box with a cardboard tube or two sticking out the end. Chances are you can create more fun toys with household items than could be purchased at the store at an exorbitant cost!

TAPE RECORDER GAMES

PROJECT SKETCH

Children find tape recorders fascinating. They love listening to sounds and guessing what they are. They like to record their own voices, and develop sound effects. Since tape recorders are fun, children effortlessly develop listening and observation skills which help form the foundation for later communication development.

HOW-TO

Here are two ways to use a tape recorder to develop communication skills:

1. **Listening and sound identification.** When your child is not present, take the tape recorder around the house and record the sounds of everyday events. Be creative! The blender, microwave oven timer, door shutting, toilet flushing, doorbell ringing, bird singing, or car starting. Take the tape recorder on errands, recording sirens, cash registers, and sounds at a construction site. Record as many sounds as you can, and make a game of identifying them. Help your child recognize emotion in the voice without the benefit of seeing facial expressions. Record happy voices, sad voices, and angry voices. Record friends, family, and television programs, making a game of helping your child identify them.

2. **Recording your child's voice.** Record your child performing one of the other activities in this section, and play it back for him. He will begin to reflect on and adjust his speech behavior as he becomes accustomed to the sound of his own voice. Develop some

structured activities as well; maybe your child can listen to some radio advertisements and develop some of his own.

Encourage your child to "just play" with the tape recorder to enhance creativity.

TIMELY TIP

Use the recordings of voices to discuss *emotions* heard in your child's world. When in public, point out emotional displays such as a crying child at the grocery store and speculate with your child on why the person feels that way.

FUTURE ADVENTURE

For a child who is old enough to operate the tape recorder for himself, switch the "sound identification" game around. Allow *him* to record sounds for *you* to identify. Encourage him to "create" voices with different emotions which you then attempt to identify.

MAKE IT MEMORABLE!

Sound effects are a loud, crazy, creative, and fun way to improve your child's powers of observation. As mentioned previously, crinkling a piece of tin foil sounds like fireworks and banging two dried coconut halves together sounds like horses' hooves. Once he gets the hang of it, challenge your child to try recreating a wide variety of sounds.

CHAPTER FIFTEEN

AGES EIGHT TO TWELVE

Joe's parents just can't figure him out. He alternates between being loud and energetic, and quiet, almost melancholy. As he becomes more sensitive to the reactions of those around him, he sometimes seems more uncomfortable with close physical contact from his parents. His mother wonders what is going on inside, but Joe isn't really able, or willing, to tell her. What is happening?

The time between ages eight and twelve may be an awkward growing time for your child. The good news is that communication activities serve as a fantastic antidote to some of the complications that pre-adolescents face. Let's assume that we know Joe well enough to diagnose what is happening in his life (these struggles are actually quite common for children this age):

- Joe's incredible growth spurt leaves him feeling gangly and awkward.

- As Joe tries to identify his place in the world, he is highly impressionable.

- Joe has a hard time describing what is going on inside.

- Joe feels uncomfortable in social situations.

- Joe feels somewhat bored by his circumstances.

Communication activities serve as a fantastic antidote to some of the complications that pre-adolescents face.

The activities in this chapter might help Joe to:

• Become more confident in his social skills.

• Develop the ability to discern good or bad influences from the world around him.

• Learn to express his feelings and thoughts more effectively.

• Find greater comfort in social situations.

• Develop more enthusiasm for life.

The building of communication skills at this age is more direct than at the three-to-seven age range. Because your child is better able to understand the commands and suggestions you give him, learning to improve is more a matter of *patience* and *practice* than of play and participation. In order to equip yourself to work with your child in this age range, consider the following overview of his likely characteristics.

WHAT WILL HE BE LIKE?

Children ages eight to twelve usually retain the terrific imagination from their younger years, but may begin turning it toward research, discovery and learning of new things. Whereas before he may have needed some help in being kept busy, your child may now be more interested in doing things with others, working with groups, and spending time with peers.

NOW YOU'RE THINKING!

L. S. Vygotsky, the Russian researcher, demonstrated that during this time period, children gain the ability to think abstractly. A phrase such as "a stitch in time saves nine" may, when explained, remind them of the virtue of prevention rather than just the skill of sewing! When you ask your child to "set the table," this will mean something other than "sit at the table." He will gradually begin to understand the abstract concepts behind the Bible stories and books you read to him, so it is a good time to focus on the character traits that heroes and role models possess.

I KNOW HOW YOU FEEL!

Although children at this age should become more sensitive to the needs of those around them, according to David Elkind, they will be most concerned about issues which have immediate impact on their lives. Politics, for example, may become more meaningful to your child as he grows older, but he is likely to reflect your political beliefs without much question. He will probably be far more concerned about his performance and the outcome of his team's performance in a baseball game. He often needs an empathetic ear, but he also needs to understand the source of his feelings and thoughts.

Moreover, your child will not yet understand the short-comings and flaws of those he respects. He is likely to imitate adult behavior without considering whether it is appropriate or wise to do so. At the same time, your child will become more proficient at distinguishing the emotions expressed by others, not only in what people say but by the tone they use. He may express concern or joy in response to the emotional reactions of others. His questions may turn from the nature of what people are like to what they believe, and what his own purpose in life entails.

HOW WELL CAN I COMMUNICATE?

Professors Allen and Brown, among the foremost experts on child speech, concluded that the following

Although children ages 8 to 12 should become more sensitive to the needs of those around them, they will likely be concerned about issues which have immediate impact on their lives.

communication characteristics will most likely define children in the eight-to-twelve age group:

- they know how to use evidence to support their claims,

- they can present persuasive arguments to support their actions,

- they can take into account another person's point-of-view if asked to do so,

- they can present and understand information that relates to objects that are not immediately visible, and

- they can understand the feedback that others give them, and can give feedback themselves.

As you begin working with your child using the activities in this chapter, you will notice improvements in his ability to:

- evaluate the messages of others and make comments about them,

- take the role of another person without being pushed to do so,

- present concepts from his own thoughts as well as those of others,

- use messages that refer to situations or ideas that are not part of his present situation, and

- adapt his messages to the needs of those who are listening.

HELPING YOUR CHILD UNDERSTAND HIS BEHAVIOR

Commenting on and reviewing situations and interactions will help your child understand his behavior. You can help your child identify what worked and what didn't in the way he spoke to and listened to another person. Professor Friedman of the University of Kansas suggests you teach him to ask, "How did that interaction turn out?" "What was the effect of that person's behavior on me?" "What was the effect of my behavior on that person?" Help your child evaluate how he feels after interacting with someone: excited or bored, secure or threatened, comfortable or uncomfortable. Ask *why* he felt that way, and enable him to understand how the unspoken behavior of the person, the circumstances, and his own expectations play a role in how he relates to others.

WHAT KIND OF ACTIVITIES WILL BE HELPFUL?

The projects in this section take advantage of the fact that your child is becoming more sensitive to his actions and how he relates to others. While the level of energy and increasing competitiveness of some children may mask their feelings, be assured that your efforts to help your child become more aware of the world around him will eventually pay off.

A word of warning: children at this age take put-downs and sarcastic language personally. Be very careful that your mood around them is controlled, and be sure your child knows that *your* emotional state is not *his* fault. In fact, if you are upset with something that does not involve the child, carefully explain the situation to him. And as always, take responsibility for your feelings: instead of saying, "That person makes me mad," emphasize that, "I do not hate that person, but I feel very frustrated when they do that."

The activities in this chapter will begin the process of giving your child the opportunity to stand and speak, although for very short periods of time and in front of limited audiences. This breaking-in period is essential for him to be comfortable in front of larger audiences and in more intense person-to-person relationships in the future.

OBSERVATION SKILLS

PROJECT SKETCH

Observation skills are the life blood of communication. We use our eyes and ears to deepen the well of experience from which we draw the life-giving waters of communication. In short, our fuel for descriptive talk comes from sharp powers of observation.

HOW-TO

You can help your child develop sharp powers of observation through a few simple activities, consistently repeated. Here is a small sampling:

1. **"If I were in your shoes."** Brainstorm a list of characteristics such as "homeless," "single mom," "angry driver," and "bully." Have your child draw a characteristic from a box and brainstorm a list of thoughts, feelings and attitudes that such a person might have, as well as some impressions of what that person might be going through. Ask, "What would Jesus do if he met that person?" If possible, engage your child in a ministry activity around this project. After a while, he will think about himself less and thus become a blessing to others.

2. **"What are they thinking?"** This game allows your child to speculate about the feelings, motives and thoughts of others. Use television and movie characters, book characters, people in news articles, and public figures. Ask questions such as, "Why do you suppose they did that?" and "What led them to act that way?"

FUTURE ADVENTURES

1. **Observation Game.** Play a game where you and your child take turns glancing at a scene (along the road or

in a picture book) for ten seconds, and then closing your eyes and listing as many things as you can that you observed.

2. **Question asking.** With the "If I were in their shoes" and "What are they thinking" games, have your child speculate on what *he* would do in that situation. This skill is important to interpersonal communication throughout life.

TIMELY TIP

Every moment is not a teachable moment! In the car, your child may prefer to play cards in the back seat or read a book than observe the world around. This is often irritating to parents, who want each trip to be "memorable." Since you cannot force him to appreciate the scenery as much as you do, be content with small doses of participation!

MAKE IT MEMORABLE!

Every family does, or should, go on lots of field trips. Where possible, invest in the trip by conducting some research in advance. For example, before visiting a sheep ranch, study sheep in the Bible, examine how shepherds live, and learn how wool is processed. Have your child call the market for the price on virgin wool, or to inquire about the cost of raising sheep. If you are planning a nature hike, help your child memorize the names and identities of a couple of trees, flowers, birds and animals you might see. On a more extensive adventure, use pre-planning as a way to generate enthusiasm. Before visiting a Civil War battle-field, for instance, read biographical stories about the Civil War and its major players or draw out a battle map. Consider checking out a wholesome movie drama or documentary about the place you are visiting.

NAMING GAMES

PROJECT SKETCH

This exercise emphasizes higher-order observation skills. Its purpose is to teach your child to use his observation skills as a springboard to imaginative description. The greatest communicators in the world are successful because of their ability to create vivid and memorable images in the minds of an audience, even getting an audience to feel personally affected by and responsible for those images.

A good case in point is Winston Churchill. Acknowledged by many as one of the greatest speakers in history, Churchill was a master of vivid description. Churchill's biographers take great pleasure in pointing out his imagination in even the most ordinary circumstances. For instance, a bulldozer Churchill once rented for landscaping his estate became stuck in the mud, and he described the plan to extricate the machine in a letter to his wife: "The animal is very strong with his hands but feeble with his caterpillar legs, and as the fields are sopping, they had the greatest difficulty in taking him away. They will have to lay down sleepers all the way from the lake to the gate over which he will waddle on Monday." Note the effort used to describe such a simple process. By investing the machine with animal-like qualities and giving it a personality, he enlivened an otherwise drab description.

How-To

The purpose of this project is to sharpen your child's ability to use his eyes to *observe* rather than just to *see*. Here are two exercises to help accomplish this goal.

1. **Encourage imaginative description.** Cut pictures out of newspapers and colorful magazines such as National

Geographic. Start with pictures of people or things with which the child is not familiar.

- People. What might this person's life have been like? Make up a story about where they grew up. List as many words as you can to describe this person.

- Objects. What is its function? What animal does it look like? How do you make it work? What would you do with it if you had one?

2. **Describe without naming.** Put the cutouts into a box, and ask the child to draw and describe one. Try to guess what is being described.

FUTURE ADVENTURE

Observe people in public. Go for a soft drink at a busy restaurant and observe people. Observe how they greet others, how they walk, and the expressions and posture they exhibit.

TIMELY TIPS

Imaginative description takes a long time to develop. Don't rush the process, but reward your child for being more coherent and fluent than he was before. You will notice an increase in descriptive ability over time.

MAKE IT MEMORABLE!

Good literature is fertile soil for growing imaginative minds. Reading to your child and encouraging him to read will help hone this skill. Classic literature is far better for this purpose than modern children's books. Standards such as *Treasure Island, The Three Musketeers,* and *Robinson Crusoe* are outstanding, not only because they have an imaginative thesis, but because they contain lessons of moral value.

VOCABULARY BUILDING

PROJECT SKETCH

Good communication skill requires words that accurately describe what you wish to convey. As language becomes more vivid, you can actually become more powerful in your speech. A healthy vocabulary also builds the foundation for the greater use of natural intelligence.

How-To

1. Pictures and objects.

- Find an object or picture that looks interesting and discuss it.

- Tell me a story about this object.

- List as many words as you can think of to describe this object.

- What are some other things like this? *How* are they like it?

- What is its purpose? How would you use it?

- What else can we use in the same way?

    For variety, make a contest out of describing the object. Choose an object that is unfamiliar to your child, such as a piece of machinery. Praise him for thinking of the funniest, most creative use. For example, the speaker cover of a transistor radio could be seen as "a computer keypad for woodpeckers," "a place to plant very small seeds," etc.

2. **Use crossword puzzles and word games.** Extend your investment in activity books beyond coloring! Choose inexpensive books at your child's age and skill level to keep him busy during "down times" at home or on trips. "Mad-Libs," for example, asks the child to create a list of descriptive words such as an action verb, emotion, color, or thing. The more descriptive the words, the funnier the resulting fill-in-the-blank story.

3. **Flash cards.** This is a time-proven means of learning new words—all the way to adulthood! When you encounter a new word, encourage your child to look it up and write the word on one side of an index card and the definition on the other. These cards can be used in a variety of ways:

   • Lay the flash cards with the words face-up. Give your child clues about each definition until he guesses all of the words correctly. Then, reverse the cards, give him the definition and ask for the correct word.

   • Time trials. Show the definition or the word, asking your child to guess it as quickly as he can. Work toward the most correct answers in the shortest time.

FUTURE ADVENTURE

Try object flash cards. Create several dozen flash cards with objects and characteristics such as "barn," "green," "happy," "fun," "car," etc. The object of the game is for the "reader" to describe the object or characteristic to the "guesser" without using the word on the card. For a more difficult game, list several *other* words which may not be used in the description.

TIMELY TIP

A child must encounter a word three times, on average, before he knows it. Point out words as they come up. By the way, the old adage "look it up for yourself" really works!

MAKE IT MEMORABLE!

Encourage your child to brainstorm pictures for each new word. We learn words most effectively when they are used colorfully, with vivid descriptions and mnemonic devices. Remember the word "distraught," for example, by picturing a lost person panicked because they are a *"distance"* from where they *"ought"* to be. It takes practice, but it really works!

NOTES

MEMORY

PROJECT SKETCH

Memory skills are integrally related to communication. A sharp memory will help your child become a clearer thinker and a more interesting conversationalist. It will prepare him for the memorized outlines which are essential to a good speech, and if he memorizes material with solid moral content, he will have a much deeper message to communicate.

HOW-TO

In this exercise, we will focus on two unique ways to heighten your child's skills of memorization.

1. **Enhance Bible memory options.** Alice Chapin, in her book *Building Your Child's Faith*, suggests the following activities:

   A. **Use a quiz.** "I am thinking of a verse in _____ referring to a _____." Give your child hints while he looks it up in the Bible. You might even try sketching clues in the form of pictures, or play Bible verse "Pictionary" in which one family member draws clues and the others try to guess what verse is being described.

   For instance, "The wages of sin is death, but the gift of God is eternal life in Jesus Christ our Lord" (Romans 6:23), might look like this:

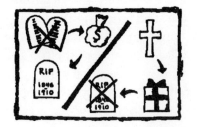

B. **Verse puzzle.** Put the verse on a card, cut into pieces with one word per piece. Put the pieces in an envelope and use the timer to see how quickly your child can assemble them correctly. For a more challenging version, put several verses together in the same envelope!

C. **Memory walk.** Write one word or a phrase on "foot prints" cut out of construction paper. The child steps from one to the other, reading as he goes. You can place verses on the floor from his room to the bathroom, from the living room to the kitchen, up and down stairs, or wherever you or your child wish to put them.

2. **Sequence and substance game.** Make up two identical sets of cards, about 50 in all. Draw a simple picture on each with a magic marker. Place one set in another room, and keep one set with you. Show your child a certain number of cards in a certain order for about 10 seconds. Have him go to the other room and pick out those same cards and place them in the same order.

Continue the competition to see how many cards he can correctly identify and place in the correct order. If he finds the task too difficult, start with just getting the right cards, working on sequence when he becomes proficient at the initial task. You can also use actual objects, giving instructions of what to do with them, in which order to put them, or how to organize them. For example, put a sack, a rubber band, a potato, and some dried beans in another room. Instruct your child to "Go to the other room, pick up the potato, put the rubber band around it, put it in the sack and add five beans. Close the sack at the top and bring it back, being sure to close the door when you return." Give praise liberally for successfully completed tasks, and make them more complex with each success.

FUTURE ADVENTURE

To help your child prepare for future speech lessons, assign poems, sayings, and quotes for him to memorize. Use them to create short speeches on several topics. A good speech makes liberal use of such tools.

TIMELY TIP

Employ memory techniques. Two commonly overlooked techniques are 1) bizarre images and 2) sequence. If you are memorizing a list, for instance, think of a bizarre representation of the objects, fitting them together in an action-oriented way. Let's say you wish to pick up four items from the grocery store: lettuce, cereal, shaving cream, and bananas. Imagine pouring cereal on a bowl of lettuce and topping it with bananas and a flourish of shaving cream.

MAKE IT MEMORABLE!

Host a friendly family competition. Alice Chapin suggests making a contract with your family for memorizing a certain number of Bible verses. If the kids win, the adults will _____. If the adults win, the kids will _____. Beware of a child's power of memory!

NOTES

LISTENING

PROJECT SKETCH

Children who become better listeners will become better learners. Studies show that better listening leads to a better vocabulary, increased comprehension and greater retention. The benefits are practical as well. Most careers require refined listening skills. This makes sense—listening is the most common form of communication. There are no tricky techniques to learning listening skills. If you as a parent are merely aware of the need, you can begin to structure your activities to emphasize listening.

HOW-TO

Here are a couple of simple ideas:

1. **Listening retention.** Read a quote, paragraph or even a whole selection from a book or magazine and ask questions about the selection. Do the same with a radio or television program.

2. **Active listening.** This involves listening carefully to what another person says to be sure you understand what they mean. You can try this by making a statement or claim and having your child ask one of two types of questions:

Questions to Restate:

"From what I hear you saying…"

"Are you saying that…"

"So from your point of view…"

"Let me restate what you are saying to make sure I understand. Are you saying that…"

"Did I understand you to say…"

"So what you're saying is…"

Questions to Reflect:

"How did that make you feel?"

"What do you think about it now?"

"How did that affect you?"

"Tell me more about it."

"I'd like to know more.

FUTURE ADVENTURES

1. **Allow your child to ask questions of you, or if you have more than one child, have your children ask questions of one another.**

2. **Play detective games.** Think of a random object (or person) and instruct your child to ask "yes" or "no" questions to guess what it is. Become increasingly obscure in the objects you choose. The goal of the game is to get your child to really listen to the clues you give and if others play, to the questions *they* ask. Through asking methodical questions, it is possible to guess virtually anything.

TIMELY TIP

Children are most likely to listen when the stimulus is varied, so alternate study periods with play periods and don't dwell on any one topic for too long.

MAKE IT MEMORABLE!

By age twelve your child should have the ability to take simple notes from a speech, a sermon, or a television or radio program. Show him a basic outline format, explain how to take down a few key words or ideas, and allow him to practice. It is a fact that most people listen much better and retain more when they take notes.

NOTES

TELL ME HOW

PROJECT SKETCH

Being able to verbally describe what we see is a key to precision as well as imagination in speech. "Tell Me How" teaches your child to give and receive directions for copying an object without being able to see the object he is copying. This exercise builds on the skills of observation and description. It emphasizes listening, and reinforces the interactive nature of communication. Through practice, your child will learn how to quickly process information and develop "common sense" about following directions. He will learn how to give directions as well, turning his observations into coherent speech.

HOW-TO

Erect a screen between you and your child (a sheet on a clothesline will do) or seat yourself and your child around the corner from one another. Build a structure out of blocks, and describe to the child what you are building, so he can build an identical structure based on your description. For additional difficulty, set rules such as, "I will only give the direction once" and "Only one question about each direction." At the end, debrief and point out how small mistakes dramatically change the outcome. You will discover that your own communication may lack precision (thus a side benefit of this exercise is the opportunity to improve communication with your child).

FUTURE ADVENTURES

1. **Have your *child* build the structure and describe it to *you*.** Also, try using paper and pencil, or crayons instead of blocks.

2. **Try a "Where Do I Go?" game.** Blindfold your child and help him negotiate an obstacle course through verbal instructions (two small steps to the left, three steps straight, etc.).

TIMELY TIPS

1. **Purposefully give incomplete instructions on occasion.** Teach your child how to recognize that he doesn't have enough information and how to ask for more by stating, "I don't understand. Can you give me more information?" He can ask more specific questions as well.

2. **Overcoming frustration.** Explain that when we feel frustrated, it is best to stay calm and practice being patient. When we are calm, the instructions seem less confusing and our attitude helps the other person be more clear. This activity, along with many of the others in this section, provides good opportunities to teach the character trait of patience.

MAKE IT MEMORABLE!

"Make a Peanut Butter Sandwich" game. This is an old, hilarious game which emphasizes the need for precise communication in giving instructions. Tell your child you want him to give you precise instructions on how to make a peanut butter sandwich. Take all of his instructions *literally*. For instance, if his first instruction is, "Put the peanut butter on the bread," take the jar of peanut butter and set it on top of the loaf. And so on.

EXPRESSIVENESS

PROJECT SKETCH

It is said that the eye is the gateway to the soul, but it would be more accurate to say that the *whole face* is the gateway to the soul. Children *at birth* have the ability to distinguish between positive and negative emotional expressions by looking at a face. The goal of this exercise is to encourage children to more accurately distinguish the emotions of others while refining their own expressiveness.

HOW-TO

Make a list of the 26 letters of the alphabet and assign one emotion and corresponding facial/body expression for each. You don't need to do *every* letter, but just enough to make the formation of several words possible. Here are some suggestions:

A = Angry, aggressive, anxious, arrogant

B = Boisterous, bashful, blissful, bored

C = Content, confident, curious

D = Disgusted, determined, disappointed, disapproving

E = Excited, enraged, envious, exasperated

F = Frightened, frustrated, fretful

G = Goody-goody, grieving, goofy

H = Happy, horrified, hurt

I = Impatient, indifferent, idiotic, innocent, interested

J = Jubilant, jealous, joyful

K = Kidding

L = Loving, lonely

M = Mean, meditative, miserable

N = Nervous

O = Obstinate, optimistic

P = Paranoid, perplexed, prudish, puzzled, proud

Q = Quiet, quizzical, quirky

R = Regretful, relieved

S = Sad, satisfied, shocked, sheepish, smug, surprised, suspicious, sympathetic

T = Thoughtful, transfixed

U = Undecided, uppity

W = Withdrawn

Make expressions yourself, and see if your child can decode them. Then let him try it!

FUTURE ADVENTURE

Try the same thing with body postures! For example, C = Confident, L = Lazy.

TIMELY TIPS

1. **Begin observing the facial expressions other people use.** When you are in public, get feedback from your child on what sorts of expressions he has noticed.

2. **Help your child think through the expressions himself.** Do not be too quick to provide an easy answer.

MAKE IT MEMORABLE!

Teach your family members to apply this exercise by becoming more sensitive to the emotional state of other family members. Instead of encouraging them to continually point out expressions to each other, impress on them the need to think about what that expression means, how the person feels, and how to respond accordingly.

NOTES

DISCUSSION

PROJECT SKETCH

Children should recognize that we get new ideas and make friends through sincere, courteous and active discussion. Through discussion we learn to understand how other people think and feel about important issues. Discussions perform the "linking" function of communication. Being able to explore ideas, listen critically and keep one's cool in a discussion will allow your child to excel in a variety of social situations.

A discussion is free-form, yet directed enough to ensure that each individual's concerns have been fully discussed, and to maintain an atmosphere of respect and courtesy.

HOW-TO

Begin with an informal and loosely-structured atmosphere. It is best to have at least three people involved. According to Professors Huckleberry and Strother, there are five basic kinds of discussion questions:

1. **Content.** "How did Moses get across the Red Sea?"

2. **Similar Experience.** "Have you ever had bad feelings toward someone?"

3. **Comparison.** "We have read another story like the one we just finished. What was the name of it?"

4. **Judgement.** "What was wrong with Adam and Eve taking and eating the fruit?"

5. **If-You-Were-There.** "If you had been on the boat with the disciples when the storm came up, what would you have done?"

FUTURE ADVENTURES

1. **Draw topics out a of a box.** Each person in the discussion can insert topics.

2. **Use puppets.** With younger children, use puppets to discuss things. Assume the identity of the puppet and express its "feelings" and "thoughts." Older children can help teach, using puppets to develop discussion skills in younger children.

3. **Tennis ball game.** Toss a ball to someone and ask him to make a statement or ask a question and then toss it to someone else. See how long you can go.

TIMELY TIP

Especially in a family environment, it is important for each member to show respect for the other members by taking turns, restating, and reflecting what the other person has just said before he can speak. Find opportunities in family meetings, family night or even during arguments to practice.

MAKE IT MEMORABLE!

Here is a technique to use during family meetings to make sure everyone s voice is heard! The speaker holds an object (a prized family souvenir or just a kitchen utensil) while he is speaking. During the time he has the object, others are not allowed to interrupt. For the sake of practice, have the other participants raise up their hands when they wish to say something. When the first speaker is finished, he can hand the object to the next speaker. This helps the discussion proceed in an orderly manner, requiring all participants to show respect for the others.

QUESTION-ASKING

PROJECT SKETCH

Children who know how to ask questions of others provide more enjoyable company and are better able to learn and absorb information. Moreover, the ability to ask good questions is seen by many as a sign of intelligence. According to Josh McDowell, scholars during Bible times demonstrated their understanding of a subject through "Rabbinical riddles," which meant answering a question with an equally well-phrased and ponderous question. Teaching your child to ask good questions is not an overnight assignment; it takes years of practice. However, here are some tips which can set your child in the right direction.

HOW-TO

Who, what, when, where and why questions may be easily taught. Set up situations, such as field trips or visits with friends, in which your child can ask them.

Here are four ways, suggested by Professors Mackay and Watson, to use questions:

1. **Recall or repeat a question asked by you.**

2. **Select an idea from a bank** (a list of questions you devise).

3. **Apply a pre-learned question in a new situation.** For example, on a field trip to a local business, ask, "What subjects did you study in school that might help you in this job?"

4. **Ask your child to think up his own ideas, and ask questions based on them.**

FUTURE ADVENTURES

1. **Interviews.** Ask a business person for some sample questions they use in employee interviews. Have your child take the lead in asking these or similar questions of family members. He most likely will need to plan questions in advance, and may need assistance in anticipating responses.

2. **Video or audio tape a mock interview situation.** By viewing or listening to himself, your child can discover areas in which he might improve. This will help make the lessons more concrete. Check the quality of questions asked (clarity and relevance) and delivery (volume and articulation).

TIMELY TIPS

1. **Prepare in advance.** If you know something about the person with whom you will be visiting, relay some details to your child that he might find interesting, or that will make the person seem less intimidating. Praise your child for a job well done!

2. **Give your child an idea of the kind of topics people like to discuss:** family, hobbies, something exciting that happened to them, a dream vacation, where they grew up, childhood memories, and the most important lesson they have learned.

3. **The best questions are open-ended, requiring more than a "yes" or "no" answer:**

   CLOSED: "Do you like the Colorado Rockies baseball team?"

   OPEN: "What sports do you enjoy watching or playing?"

Make It Memorable!

Teach your child to ask questions that refer to ideas, thoughts and feelings rather than just the immediate situation. This will help him grasp deeper concepts and build a more powerful vocabulary. Ultimately, your child will learn best from your example! When you express genuine interest in another person by asking substantive questions, you will set an enormously powerful example for your child.

NOTES

TELEPHONE SKILLS

PROJECT SKETCH

Every time you answer the telephone, you have an opportunity to make a good first impression. If the caller's impression is a good one, you have the opportunity to develop a relationship with that person. If not, your negative impression may last in their mind for years.

There are many reasons to teach telephone etiquette to your child. First, you will become more comfortable with him answering the telephone and even taking messages. Second, your child reflects you and your family in everything he does. If he is polite and communicative in telephone etiquette, one of the primary forms of communication in our culture, he will be an example of a well-taught child.

The benefit to your child is also great. He will learn to speak clearly and enthusiastically, endearing him to others throughout life.

HOW-TO

The key to telephone etiquette is devising an appropriate way to answer, and then practicing a variety of situations. The following is a standard, polite telephone greeting:

"Good morning, _____ residence, this is _____. How may I help you?"

Other rules:

- Before transferring a call to the intended recipient, always ask, "Who may I say is calling?"

- If the person being requested is not able to take the call, just say "_____ is not able to come to the phone right now. May I take a message?" Don't explain where they are. If the caller asks "Where are they?" ask in return, "Why do you ask?"

- Always take a complete message, noting the person s name with correct spelling, what the call is regarding, telephone number, date and time.

- Never tell strangers anything until they identify themselves. Even then, divulge information cautiously.

- When you are alone, never tell a stranger that your parents are not home. There is no need to lie; a simple, "He or she cannot come to the phone right now, may I take a message?" will do.

TIMELY TIPS

1. **Practice exact wording and tone of voice, and create various situations to which your child can learn to respond.** Practice what to do if callers do not want to identify themselves, what to do when you are not home, etc.

2. **Use telephone etiquette as a prerequisite to telephone privileges.** Insist that your child learn to answer the telephone properly and take messages responsibly before being allowed to call friends. It might be a good idea to establish rules for telephone use as well (i.e., time limits, number of calls per day, who may call him, etc.). Do not take for granted that your child understands things such as "no long distance calls without permission," or "no taking calls during designated family time or homework time."

MAKE IT MEMORABLE!

Be a little sneaky and use random reinforcement! Ask your friends to call and test your child at random intervals and report the results to you. Offer some sort of small prize or privilege for success.

NOTES

"DESCRIBE A PROCESS" SPEECH

PROJECT SKETCH

This project will familiarize your child with the sequential structure of a speech. Structure (a sense of before, during and after) is what makes the speech experience possible. Even though your child's experience with the world is still limited, he can learn to construct meaning from events, and use this as the basis for conveying thoughts in an orderly manner.

HOW-TO

This speech is like an oral report used to debrief activities. After you visit a factory, for instance, ask your child to rehearse the process through which the product is made. He may need some assistance in discerning the most important features of the process. After visiting a logging mill, for example, he can give a speech about how trees are turned into lumber. This is done by dividing the process into three or four identifiable, easy-to-remember steps.

Have your child organize the speech by giving an overview, explaining the main points and then concluding with a review. As the old speech coach advised, "Tell them what you are going to tell them, tell them, and then tell them what you told them." At this age, you can begin requiring increasingly rigorous standards of delivery and organizational skill. This means, for starters, that the introduction of the speech should capture the attention of the audience. For the logging speech, it might be:

Imagine yourself on a construction site. You hear the pounding of hammers, the buzz of a saw, and the voice of the foreman shouting instructions to the crew. All of a sudden, a large truck pulls up with an enormous load of freshly cut lumber. The smell is sweet, almost like being in a forest. We see construction projects all the time but rarely stop to consider how we get construction lumber from trees. I recently visited a saw mill and observed the process. Basically, there are three steps…

Good speeches also have an appropriate conclusion, which might be something like this:

So the next time you sit on a wooden deck, or go to a lumber yard and smell the fresh smells, or pound a nail, think of all of the steps in the process from the tree to me.

FUTURE ADVENTURE

Try an "impressions speech." Have your child describe his *impressions* of a process he has observed. What was particularly memorable and why? Praise him for accuracy and colorful descriptions.

TIMELY TIPS

1. **Help your child focus on the *process* rather than on the specific details.** If your child has watched a movie and is describing it to someone else, the most important thing is not the funny scenes which stand out in his mind, but what the story was *about*.

2. **Ask lots of "why" questions, such as, "Why did the men in the lumber mill wear hard hats?"**

3. **If your child is having difficulty getting the steps in the right order, jot them down.** This will help him see the correct order in a more objective way, so that if the details are out of order, the main point is still clear. This is actually the first step in learning to take outline notes.

MAKE IT MEMORABLE!

Allow your child to help establish the plans for a family outing. Then ask him to brief the family on the plans for the day in three or four identifiable steps. Take turns as family members.

NOTES

DEMONSTRATION SPEECH

PROJECT SKETCH

The age range from eight to twelve is a good time for your child to move from just relating experiences to doing so in a disciplined manner. As Professors Huckleberry and Strother note, speaking formally will help him refine his thoughts and feelings and reconstruct them in the light of previous failures. A demonstration speech is a good place to start, because your child can rely on props as the center of attention. Demonstration speeches focus on process, identifying the steps necessary to complete a task. This skill is vital to any future success in speech making or story telling.

HOW-TO

Begin with giving a speech about a process in which the child has recently engaged. For instance, if he has learned how to make ice cream in a churn, have him demonstrate the process in identifiable steps. Make sure the speech is complete with an introduction:

I. Introduction.

"I scream, you scream, we all scream for ice cream! Eating ice cream is such a popular thing to do in America that it could probably be called a 'great American pastime.' The problem, however, is that buying ice cream in the store is so expensive. How would you like to learn a way of making ice cream that only costs about 25 cents a serving, is more tasty, and far more healthy than store-bought ice cream? It is as simple as following these three steps."

II. Point 1: Assemble materials.

III. Point 2: Mix ingredients.

IV. Point 3: Stir them in an ice cream churn.

V. Conclusion.

FUTURE ADVENTURES

Try other speeches with a similar structure such as the "three reasons" speech. "Three reasons why I would like to go camping this weekend," or "Three reasons why I am upset with Joe."

TIMELY TIPS

1. **Be persistent!** Giving speeches in the home may seem awkward, but the only way to learn is to practice. All successful speakers rehearse at home and in their hotel room before each important speech.

2. **Focus on careful speech.** Have your child concentrate on speaking slowly and carefully. There is no rush to finish, and speaking somewhat deliberately is a sign of mature speech.

3. **Focus on posture.** Formal and informal speech is often distinguished by posture. Have your child stand straight—with his shoulders back, although not unnaturally so. The important thing about posture is that the your child should stand in such a way as to express confidence. He can also begin improving his hand gestures and facial expressions.

MAKE IT MEMORABLE!

Use speeches to create a positive atmosphere in your home. Reminisce about shared memories and anticipate future family experiences. You can do this through the "three things I like" speech. For example, "Three things I like about Grandpa," or "Three things I am looking forward to at the fair."

NOTES

MYSTERY PROJECTS

PROJECT SKETCH

This project shows you how to increase your child's interest in speech through suspense, enthusiasm, and curiosity. It is not as much a specific speech activity as an exciting way for your child to learn communication skills without thinking about it. These activities reinforce the need for creating curiosity, building it, sustaining it and fulfilling it.

HOW-TO

1. **Mystery letter.** Write and send your child an "anonymous" letter with strange characteristics such as misspelled words, smeared with something that forms a clue. Include a clue or promise a reward if he performs a certain task, such as memorizing a certain Bible verse or poem, putting it on tape and burying it in a designated spot. You can continue the project or add creative variations as you wish.

2. **Treasure hunt.** Have a "pirate" hide a treasure with a clue hidden on a piece of map paper in the chapter of a book your child is assigned to read. You could reward his work with pieces of a map so that after the completion of a set number of tasks he can find the treasure.

FUTURE ADVENTURES

1. **Use video or audio tape to record the messenger's voice and the child's response.** Be expressive, and encourage your child's expressiveness.

2. **Ask your friends to help.** You probably have some friends who are good enough sports to dress up in

costumes for a mystery project. Even a slight disguise will throw your child off their scent.

TIMELY TIP

Make *learning* a requirement for solving the mystery. At the same time, do not make the tasks so difficult as to discourage the child from trying. Also, use creative mystery sparingly. Otherwise you will run yourself ragged trying to conceive new ideas, and your child may become bored. These projects are best used to "spice up" a topic during a learning dry spell.

MAKE IT MEMORABLE!

Invite special guests. If you know people who are knowledgeable about the subjects your child is studying, invite them to visit. For instance, during a study of a war, find a war veteran who will come visit, preferably someone your child will know. They can send an old picture or photocopy of a newspaper article, anonymously, saying "I was there at the battle of _____. To find out more about it, read the encyclopedia." All the clues come together when the person arrives to give a presentation and answer questions.

CHAPTER SIXTEEN

AGES THIRTEEN AND UP

By age thirteen, the seeds you have planted over a lifetime will begin to bear fruit in your child's life. To many parents, this is a highly discouraging prospect! Don't despair. The teen years are often marked by an awkward transition into adulthood. While steady, fast improvement in communication ability is certainly not the norm in teenagers, you can expect that activities such as those in this section will help your child emerge as an articulate, graceful young adult.

During the period starting at about age thirteen, your child will reach the most advanced level of communication. Thus, this chapter will focus on all kinds of skills required of an excellent communicator, from critical thinking to the ability to "think on your feet." In order to give you an idea of why the activities in this section have been chosen as they have, let's take an inventory of what a socially adept adolescent should be able to do communicatively.

TRAITS OF A SOCIALLY-ADEPT ADOLESCENT

I know what you're thinking: "What if my teen doesn't measure up?" Don't worry. First, these traits are goals to strive for, not measures of intelligence. Second, the very fact that you and your teen are focusing on these skills will put him ahead of others his age. Incidentally, if your teen is experiencing great difficulty in any of these areas, review

Ironically,

during the very

time of their

lives when

teens are

yearning for

independence,

parental

influence and

involvement is

increasingly

vital.

the related projects in the section on eight-to-twelve-year-olds to strengthen his foundation.

Here are some expectations that the projects in this section are designed to meet:

- **Interpersonal skills.** A socially-adept teenager should know how to greet others and have a conversation with them. He should be able to recognize the feelings and emotions of others, and express accurate emotions himself. He should also know how to communicate *acceptance* to other people.

- **Ability to research and organize information.** Your teen will need to know his way around a library, become proficient at using a set of encyclopedias, and discover how to look up information in periodicals, on CD-Rom, and on the Internet. I have included an exercise in library research in this section as a means of bringing attention to this vital skill.

- **How to phrase thoughts.** As an adolescent, it will be important for your child to know how to organize and express his thoughts. He needs to be able to answer a question with "This is what I think and here's why" type answers.

- **Critique information.** According to the National Assessment of Educational Progress, nearly 40 percent of 13-year-olds lack the ability to locate information or make generalizations based on what they read. It is even more important that your child, as he enters the teen years, be able to recognize the good and bad elements of information he is exposed to. Critical inquiry takes advantage of a teen's natural inquisitiveness and argumentativeness. As Douglas Wilson states in *Recovering the Lost Tools of Learning*, "If you encourage disagreement for disagreement's sake, then you will get disagreeable children. But if you teach them that it is good to question (provided the questioning is intellectually rigorous and honest), then you are *educating*."

- **Exercise well-developed delivery skills.** During the teen years, you will begin expecting your child to act like an adult. Being able to demonstrate eye contact, energetic body language and vocal enthusiasm will be important for your teen to interact in an adult world, especially in speaking situations.

- **Understand persuasion.** In order to critically evaluate the world around them, as well as to make an effective speech, your child will need to know what makes a message persuasive and how to create persuasive messages himself.

WHAT IS MY ROLE AS A PARENT?

Frankly, the question most parents ask about teens is not, "How do I teach my teen to communicate," but, "How do I communicate with my teen?" Ironically, during the very time of teen's lives when they are yearning for independence, parental influence and involvement is increasingly vital. Do not make the erroneous assumption that because your child is growing up, he does not need as much love, understanding and acceptance. In fact, he may need more.

What is a parent's role in the life of a teenager as it regards communication skill development?

1. **Continue to challenge your teen.** As a parent, you have the opportunity to give your teen a broad base of experience during his teen years. You can continue to provide him with a challenging environment, help him develop new goals, and encourage him to improve his communication skills.

2. **Help your teen discover his purpose in life.** I am told that the number one fear of adolescents is that they will not discover their purpose in life. As a parent, you can continue to encourage your teen in this pursuit, allowing him to explore various trades, hobbies and interests. According to Dr. Ross Campbell in *Kids Who Follow, Kids Who Don't*, having one or two well-defined areas of interest will help a teen avoid the boredom that often leads to a disastrous teen experience.

3. **Listen to your teen.** It will take work to understand the messages your teen is giving and the feelings he is experiencing. It is almost impossible for us to remember our teen years well enough to identify with our own teenage children. Dr. Kathryn Koch suggests that interacting with your teens requires a lot of "active listening." To that end, she offers "clarifying comments" that create communication with teens. Here are some sample clarifying comments:

- "So what you're saying is _____. Right?"

- "You feel I'm being unfair because none of your friends have the same rule."

- "You sound like you find that assignment boring."

- "You seem to feel left out and lonely because it is hard to make friends at the new church."

- "How do you feel about what happened?"

- "What is your reason for saying (or doing) this?"

- "Can you give me an example of what you mean?"

- "What else can you tell me that will help me under-stand?"

- "What's the most important part of what you're telling me?"

It is important to note that listening in this way does not obligate you to believe and give your assent to everything your teen says and does. However, it does give you a way to make sure he knows you are *really listening*. He recognizes that he is important to you, that you trust him, and that he can continue to communicate with you.

4. **Communicate acceptance.** It is all too easy, in your effort to challenge your child, to give him the impres-sion that you will not accept him unless he conforms to your expectations. This is potentially disastrous, especially if your expectations are not clear. As a high school student, Justin Swets surveyed his classmates and discovered that there are five messages that every teen desperately wants to hear. These five messages are recorded by his father, Paul Swets, in *How to Talk so Your Teenager Will Listen*. These should come through loud and clear on a regular basis:

- "I'm proud of you." This encourages your teen to set high goals and creates a strong desire to reach them. It communicates that you are on his side, win or lose.

- "You can always come to me with anything and I will listen and try to understand." Your communica-tion with your teenager will be his lifeline through difficult times. In order to earn the right to hear him, work on giving him your undivided attention, use clarifying comments, do not ridicule him, and do your best to understand.

- "I want to understand you." This will motivate your teen to keep trying to communicate with you even if it is a struggle.

- "I trust you." The teen years are the perfect time to establish an "elevator" of trust and responsibility, a system where your teen earns freedoms when he can demonstrate a mature ability to take responsibility. Communicate to your child that there are clear ways to gain additional trust. Outline the system you choose for him so he can set goals based on it.

- "I love you." Dr. Ross Campbell notes with sadness that the very time when children need an increasing amount of love and acceptance is usually the very time where we begin to deny it to them. It never hurts to say, "I love you." Your love may be the anchor which holds your teen firm in a restless sea of ungodly philosophies and temptations.

TAKE ADVANTAGE OF REAL WORLD OPPORTUNITIES

There are a multitude of opportunities for teenagers to develop communication skills. The organizations listed here will give your teen practice, assistance, and most important, an audience.

1. **4-H Clubs.** If you live in rural America, 4-H Clubs offer an excellent opportunity for the development of communication and leadership skills. Your child will be able to participate in and run meetings by a strict parliamentary system and give demonstration speeches at contests; he will learn to try out new things and develop talents in new areas. Contact the county extension office in your county (or parish).

2. **Toastmasters, Jr.** Toastmasters is a "civic organization," their stated goal being to help members of the community improve their speech skills. Many Toastmasters clubs have now established a junior club, so high school students can learn the same skills. Look in the Yellow Pages under "community organizations" to see if a chapter has been formed in your community.

3. **Contests sponsored by civic organizations.** Civic organizations are a part of nearly every community. Many of them take the responsibility for encouraging leadership development in young people, especially in the area of speech. The Optimist Club International sponsors speech contests, judged by club members, in which any student age 12 to 16 may participate. The topic usually calls for a four-minute motivational speech (ie., "Destiny: Choice or Chance?"). Another organization to contact is the American Legion, whose speech contests offer college scholarships and the opportunity to advance to a national tournament. Again, check the Yellow Pages for "Civic Organizations" or "Community Organizations."

4. **Bible clubs.** Child Evangelism Fellowship hosts *Christian Youth in Action* programs in nearly every state. These programs train teens during a ten-week seminar to run "Five-day Clubs," summer Bible clubs for neighborhood children. For additional information, contact C. E. F. in Warrenton, Missouri.

5. **Church school, Sunday school or children's youth clubs (such as AWANA).** Nearly every church is looking for teenagers to assist in teaching younger children. Your teen will have the opportunity to give lessons, conduct puppet shows, and generally be a positive influence in the life of a younger child.

6. **Speeches at Civic Organizations.** Many civic organizations are willing to listen to speeches by young people at their meetings. These organizations include the Optimist Club, Rotary Club, Lions Club, Jaycees, Kiwanis, Sertoma, Disabled American Veterans, Serenity Club, Christian Businessmen's Committee, Women Aglow, American Legion, Veterans of Foreign Wars, International Association of Business Communicators, military club gatherings, political party meetings, and senior citizens clubs. Your teen should contact them when he has a speech already developed, and offer to come speak whenever they cannot find a speaker or have a last-minute cancellation. One national leader I know started his career in leadership by impressing community leaders through speaking to these associations. Check the Yellow Pages for organizations in your area, and have your teen write them a letter describing his speech topic and asking for the opportunity to present it. You never know what might happen!

Speeches for these organizations should focus on a teenager's perspective on an issue, stories about people who have overcome great difficulties, or book reviews (reading and then drawing out important lessons for those who might not have time to read).

7. **Mission trips.** Many missionary organizations offer short-term missions which give young people the opportunity to travel, teach, evangelize and participate in building projects. Some of these organizations encourage young people to learn drama and mime as a way of communicating across language barriers. What an excellent way to accomplish several of your goals for your child, while building strong communication skills in the process!

The teenage years are a fantastic time to build communication skills. The ability to communicate fluently and in a socially appropriate way will smooth the transition to adulthood for your teen. Perseverance on your part, even through the rough times, will be rewarded by the emergence of a confident communicator.

NOTES

GETTING TO KNOW THE LIBRARY

PROJECT SKETCH

It has often been said that, "If you want to be a leader, you've got to be a reader." Leaders are masters of great ideas, and great ideas come largely from reading. This exercise is only indirectly related to communication skills, but it reinforces critical thinking skills and sets your teen on the path to discovering something worthwhile on which to speak!

It is wise to have a personal collection of good books, as well as subscriptions to newspapers, newsletters and magazines. It is also important to visit a library for about two hours each week. One hour should be spent culling through periodicals from that week and month; the other should be spent on a research project. Assist your teen in brainstorming a topic that interests him and then assign research goals.

HOW-TO

1. **Make an appointment with the librarian for a tour.** You will discover resources you didn't know existed! Most libraries carry microfilm and microfiche records of newspapers a hundred years old, pictures of your town, historical records, and computer access programs which connect the library's computer to larger research facilities. Be sure to spend time playing with the computer access terminals if available, or perusing the card catalog or *Readers Guide to Periodical Literature*.

2. **Invent research games which will require your teen to be creative in his search for information.** Have the librarian help you discover an obscure fact (see

the example below) as well as clues as to how it might be discovered by your teen. Like a trivia game, each clue should be successively easier, the goal being to discover the information with as few clues as possible. Devise a point system to reward his perceptiveness. Here is an example taken from *Can You Find It?*, a clever book full of library scavenger hunts.

> *"Knowing I lov'd my books, he furnish'd me, from mine own library with volumes that I prize above my duke-dom." This quotation is taken from what famous play?*

> *Clue 1. What you need is a violent brainstorm — a sort of tempest of the temporal lobes, as it were.*

> *Clue 2. Shakespeare and Bartlett's...what a pear.*

> *Answer: Shakespeare's play "The Tempest," the quote found in* Bartlett's Familiar Quotations.

FUTURE ADVENTURE

Research something in-depth, such as the history of your town. Examine historical records, old newspapers, and interviews with old-timers. Choose a project which requires you and your teen to use a wide variety of resource materials. When in high school, I researched the history of the railroad in our town, read old newspapers on microfilm, interviewed a retired railroad employee, and took slides of local landmarks. This project will make an excellent presentation to community organizations, and it can also be a great parent/child or family activity.

TIMELY TIPS

Make use of many different kinds of resources: newspapers, magazines, microfilm, books, and reference tools.

Remember: in research, it's not what you know but how much access you have to what is known by others!

MAKE IT MEMORABLE!

Try a library scavenger hunt. Scavenger hunts are a common party theme, but you can throw your party-goers a curve by making a bit of library research part of yours. Find some obscure piece of trivia which forms the clue to something else. Be careful to reinforce the library's rules (maybe subtract points for those who run or are loud in the library). It is an off-beat idea—will teens go for it? They might! It just depends on how badly they want to solve the puzzle and win the competition!

NOTES

CRITICAL INQUIRY

PROJECT SKETCH

The purpose of this project is to 1) give your teen four key questions he can use to critically analyze difficult and complex issues, and 2) introduce the idea of analyzing the media. This project is not intended to make your teen argumentative, but to teach him how to get to the heart of a matter. A polite persistent argument can be a good educational experience.

HOW-TO

1. Teach your teen the key questions to critical inquiry:

- *"What do you mean by _____?"* Always ask for a definition of the key terms. Socrates said, "If you wish to debate with me, you must first of all define your terms."

- *"How do you know that to be true?"* Always question how a particular fact is known. Most people blindly miss this step, and assume that because a statement is made in a factual way, it must be true.

- *"Where do you get your information?"* What is the source of the fact in question, and can it be verified? Much of what the media calls factual is based on dubious "studies," or shallow analysis of issues. The key to the ultimate success of this question is intensive library research.

- *"What happens if you are wrong?"* Most people don't like to think that they might be wrong, but you must ask what is at stake in holding the position they do.

2. **Analyze the news.** Begin with editorials or letters to the editor which are hostile to your family's beliefs. Your teen can use the above four questions as tools of analysis to uncover flaws in reasoning. If he has difficulty, reveal some of the red flags a particular piece raises for you. Ask the following questions: Which sides are presented? Who are the sources and how are they characterized? What is the tone of the report? What underlying assumptions does the news story hold? How is an action described? What statistics are used? What is *left out* of the news story? What words, negative or positive, are used to describe the incident, people involved, position taken, or emotions expressed?

FUTURE ADVENTURE

Rewrite the headlines and news articles. For example, Ruth Beechick suggests you select a headline about your town's sports team to rewrite as the headline might have appeared in the town of the other team.

TIMELY TIP

Analyze the differences between news articles and editorials. Clip out articles and editorials on the same topic. What is the difference between the two? Outline the arguments used by the editorial writer, and compare them to the article. Is the article completely neutral?

MAKE IT MEMORABLE!

Advance your family's skills of critical inquiry by finding a book at the library on logical fallacies. A logical fallacy is an argument that appears to be logical but is actually illogical. Consider, for example, the fallacy of "ad hominem," meaning "to the man." This is an argument which tries to stop the discussion through a personal attack, such as when a secular humanist dismisses Christians as "extreme right-wing fundamentalists." There are dozens of logical fallacies which may be studied and even posted in your home to help you analyze the flaws in newspaper articles, editorials, editorial cartoons, and television news reports.

NOTES

ADVANCED LISTENING SKILLS

PROJECT SKETCH

The ability to listen to others is a sign of maturity. This project introduces advanced listening skills which your teen can exercise in observing the world around him.

HOW-TO

The goal of this exercise is to practice listening skills in two contexts: during a speech and during a one-on-one conversation.

1. **Listening to a speech.** We indicate our listening skill by our ability to recall what was said. Humans can absorb information three to ten times faster than a speaker can present it, so our minds tend to wander during speeches unless we exercise self-discipline. The best way to teach your teen to listen to a speaker is to have him take notes. Encourage him to write down the main thrust of the speech, the main points used to support it, one or two words which remind him of the supporting evidence used, and comments about the mannerisms and speaking style exhibited by the speaker, good and bad. Take notes yourself, and review with your teen after the speech.

2. **Listening in conversation.** There are at least six definable steps to being a good listener in a conversation: Be attentive, Show interest, Reflect back, Clarify, Re-state everything, and Summarize. To examine these steps in detail, refer to the chapter earlier in this book on helping your child relate to others. This process takes a long time, and is rarely carried through to completion. However, it will help

your teen understand the process more clearly if you deliberately go through the steps, practicing a response even if it seems silly.

For purposes of feedback, review the listening rules with your teen before going into a conversational setting. Check each other's listening behavior and offer feedback.

FUTURE ADVENTURE

Look for opportunities for you and your teen to practice listening skills. Volunteer to provide child care at a public event (younger children love to talk, but just need someone to listen), participate as a counselor at an evangelistic crusade, learn peer counseling skills, volunteer at a crisis pregnancy center or crisis hotline, or sign up for the visitation team at your church.

TIMELY TIP

Listening may require your family to set new priorities. Even if it takes a great deal of self-control to listen actively, resolve to always *listen* to people rather than brushing them aside. Resolve in advance that you will listen patiently. The resulting patience will develop deeper character in both parent and teen.

MAKE IT MEMORABLE!

Present listening to your family as a key to gaining wisdom. Proverbs 1:5 says, "Let the wise listen and add to their learning." We can learn something from everyone, no matter how irrelevant it seems at the time. Create a climate in your family where you are known by others as good listeners, and reinforce the process by thinking about the wisdom gained in listening.

INTERVIEW

PROJECT SKETCH

Interviewing is a highly useful way to gain information. It involves telephone and/or face-to-face encounters with those who might be informed about an issue, or with those who can give a sampling of public opinion. You can give your teen some basic interviewing skills in a short period of time, and in so doing, give him opportunities to gain courage and astuteness.

Refer, if necessary, to the "Question-Asking" project in the section for children ages eight to twelve, in which we discussed how to formulate questions to ask in a conversational setting. Below, I have suggested two specific projects which you might use or modify to give your teen the opportunity to gain interviewing experience.

HOW-TO

1. **Interview an elected official.** Call the office of an elected official and arrange to have an interview. Express to the official or to the assistant what kinds of questions you would like to ask (i.e., that you are studying how government operates and want to know more about what they do). Prepare the questions in advance.

2. **Surveys.** Any time you are studying a particular issue, conduct a survey of the public. For example, if you are studying the history of communism, put together a survey which asks people, "Is communism dead?" as well as other related questions. Your teen can conduct the surveys anywhere: the public park, city hall, or a local mall (most malls are privately owned, so check with the management office first). The value of this

exercise is that you get a clearer idea of what people are thinking about the issue. Moreover, your teen learns to be bold in approaching total strangers and communicating with them, and he also gets interesting material for a speech. You might need to help your teen write questions objectively. For example, if he is assembling a survey on abortion, your teen should ask, "Are you for or against abortion?" rather than "Are you for or against killing babies?"

FUTURE ADVENTURE

For an extra assignment, your teen can call the local newspaper and talk them into letting him write a "special editorial" from a teen perspective on the elected official he will be interviewing. When the official discovers that your teen has been "commissioned" by the newspaper, an interview will almost certainly be granted! Note: While representing the newspaper is an exciting option for this project, keep in mind that it will change the dynamic of the interview, and the elected official may be more cautious and hard to get to know personally.

TIMELY TIPS

1. **Be willing to do whatever you ask your teen to do!** Accompany him on the interviews and surveys—at least at first. He should learn to do it by himself eventually.

2. **Interviews are a good time to practice active listening.** Review some of the listening principles before you go.

3. **Watch television news reporters conducting interviews, and critique them.** What did they do right or wrong.

MAKE IT MEMORABLE!

Use interviews to reinforce your teen's sense of purpose in life. The following variation on the public opinion poll was suggested by Beverly Norsworthy, a teacher from New Zealand. She assigns students the topic of "How God has been good to me." They interview their parents and grandparents, and assemble in the process a clearer understanding of how God has worked through history to affect each of their lives.

NOTES

BEING ASSERTIVE

PROJECT SKETCH

As your child enters his teen years, it is vital that he learn to communicative assertively, especially in saying *no* when enticed to do something that is either wrong or would reflect wrong priorities. Assertiveness will help your teenager recognize when someone is trying to manipulate him, and know how to counter it.

HOW-TO

You can teach your teen this skill through role plays, where you or another teen serve as the helper. Role plays should be conducted imagining that both people are equal, that one is not the authority figure.

1. Saying no. Create a situation in which the helper is trying to manipulate your teen into doing something wrong (i.e., underage drinking). The helper's pressure should become increasingly intense, and so should the answers by your teen. Here is an example (Asserter remarks are in italics):

    1. Will you help me write my paper?
       No, that would be cheating.

    2. Come on, please?
       No.

    3. Just say yes. I need your help.
       No.

    4. Why not?
       I have said no three times, and I am getting irritated with your pressuring me. Will you please stop asking me?

5. I asked you why not.
   I gave you my reason; it would be cheating.

6. Pretty please?
   I said no. If that does not satisfy you, then I will end the conversation. Is that the only option you are leaving me with?

7. Without your helping me, I'll fail. You don't want me to fail, do you?
   Are you trying to make me feel guilty?

8. No, I just thought we were friends.
   Are you saying that unless I do what you want, I am not your friend?

9. No. Oh well, just forget it.
   Gladly. Let's change the subject.

NOTE: The asserter is under no obligation to explain his answer beyond his initial reason unless he chooses to do so. The goal is to be consistent in the answer, and aggressive in not allowing the other person to manipulate.

FUTURE ADVENTURE

Try other role plays such as refusing to take drugs or use alcohol, go to an inappropriate movie, help in a worthy, but time-consuming cause, skip work to do something fun, or neglect homework to goof around.

TIMELY TIP

Persevere! Role plays are difficult because participants often feel giggly or uncomfortable at first. Keep going until you get some results.

MAKE IT MEMORABLE!

Make this technique an integral part of teaching your children values and character. For each character quality, think of an opposing force that will try to destroy it (e.g., sexual purity vs. premarital sex). Help your teen recognize the forces at play and how to counter them.

NOTES

BEING PERSISTENT

PROJECT SKETCH

Persistence is a vital character quality for a confident communicator. Your teen must know how to ask directly for what he wants, without manipulating, and stick with it until he gets a straight answer. This does not mean "nagging" someone or trying to trick or bribe them into doing what he wants. Instead, it encourages healthy ideas of persuasion.

HOW-TO

In this role play, the helper tries to avoid saying yes to a request that is honest and direct. He sidetracks, gives very indirect "no's" and tries to change the subject. The asserter persists until he gets a direct response. Try role plays asking the person to participate in a church drama, working with him on a project, or doing an assignment that has been required of them both.

Here is an example of how it might work. (Asserter remarks are in italics):

1. *Will you participate in the church drama this year?*
   Well, I don't know.

2. *We could really use your help. What do you say?*
   Where is it going to be held?

3. *At the church. Will you help?*
   The acoustics in there are pretty bad.

4. *The acoustics won't affect what I am asking you to do. Will you help?*
   How much time will it take?

5. *About an hour and a half each day for a month. I would like to have your help.*
Speaking of dramas, did you see the new movie at the theater?

6. *I have asked you three times, and you haven't given me a direct answer yet. Will you give me a direct answer?*
Well, hmmm.

7. *Is that a yes or a no?*
I'm not sure. I'll have to think about it.

8. *Okay. May I check back tomorrow?*
Yes, that would be fine.

Notice that the asserter didn't demand a "yes," but he *did* insist on a direct answer. The asserter should not pressure or plead, or act in any way as if he expects a "yes" answer.

TIMELY TIP

Practice non-verbal communication. Your teen and the helper should sit forward rather than slouch, and maintain eye contact.

FUTURE ADVENTURE

Write out several situations to try as a family or with a group of teens. Put them in a box to draw from. Each person should take a turn as the asserter and as the helper.

MAKE IT MEMORABLE!

Learn how to recognize manipulation. Manipulation is attempting to get someone to do what *you* want by making them feel guilty. It is one of the most unhealthy forms of communication because it is almost always selfish, having no concern for the interests or feelings of the other person. Manipulative people are usually afraid of being rejected or have found manipulation to be an effective means of getting what they want. As "teachable moments" arise, show your child how communication can be manipulative. For instance, role play what to do if a friend of your child says, "If you're my friend, you'll do it." or "What are you, a chicken?" Your child should be able to respond with, "I am your friend, but I will not do what you ask." or "I think you are calling me a chicken because you can't think of another way to get me to do something that I don't want to do."

NOTES

COMMONPLACES

PROJECT SKETCH

"Commonplaces" are the secret behind the incredible memory and speech powers of ancient Greek and Roman orators. A commonplace is a means of organizing and remembering a speech by picturing in one's mind the segments of the speech as the "commonplaces" in a house. Through time the term "commonplaces" has evolved to refer to short "mini-speeches" which are pieced together in various combinations to form longer speeches. Cicero is said to have used this technique to memorize three-hour-long speeches word-for-word!

HOW-TO

Use the "commonplaces" technique to help your teen speak more confidently and to give him something to contribute on a variety of topics. Follow these steps:

1. Format.

   I. Introduction. A short statement about the topic at hand. *"One of the most important traits of a leader is that he has the courage to say what needs to be said and do what needs to be done."*

   II. Quotation. A memorable comment by a memorable character. *"We need leaders like Winston Churchill. He refused to give in, even when it looked as if Germany would certainly win. He said, 'We shall go on to the end. We shall never surrender.' His courage motivated the people to press on."* An alternative is to tell a story or give an illustration.

   III. Bible verse. *"Many times in the Bible, God encouraged his chosen leaders to have courage. He told Joshua four times to 'Be strong and courageous for the Lord thy God is with thee.'"*

IV. Concluding remark. *"Next time you face a difficult situation, remember that God will give you the courage you need to do the right thing."*

2. Choose character-building topics for commonplaces: courage, honesty, trust, kindness, mercy, integrity, vision, perseverance, responsibility, and others.

3. Use books of quotations and a Bible concordance to find quotes to memorize.

4. Your teen should be able to develop at least one new commonplace each week and recite it when called on, even on the spur of the moment. He should also be able to combine two or three related commonplaces to make a short speech.

FUTURE ADVENTURE

Use commonplaces to stimulate conversation. Much of this book focuses on conversational communication skills. When having a conversation with someone, you and your teen can use your quotes or Bible verses to encourage them.

TIMELY TIP

Don't be afraid to use humorous quotations or even a humorous approach to the ideas at hand. This will be good practice when it comes time for your teen to start giving speeches in public. Humor is greatly appreciated by an audience, and the ability of a speaker to use it confidently will depend on how familiar they are with his material.

FOR THE RECORD: "Humor" which makes fun of who people are (i.e., their nationality, race, physical infirmity, or mental deficiency) is not funny. To get laughs at the expense of the way God created someone is to mock God. Instead, good humor should be based on cleverness: laughing at yourself, telling a story with a cleverly constructed punch line, or surprising your audience with the unexpected.

MAKE IT MEMORABLE!

Use the commonplaces technique to supplement Bible memory. Surround each verse memorized with a commonplace to put it in context and perhaps make memory easier. Each verse becomes a ready-made tool of encouragement!

NOTES

IMPROMPTU SPEECHES

PROJECT SKETCH

The word "impromptu" means "without preparation or advance thought." An impromptu speech is one given off-the-cuff. We have all, on occasion, been asked to stand up and give our ideas, or even been pushed to the podium with cries of, "Speech! Speech!" The impromptu speech project will give your teen excellent practice at thinking on his feet. He will learn to speak confidently and thoughtfully in public, whether or not the situation requires a speech.

HOW-TO

1. **Format.** An impromptu speech for this exercise should be at least one minute but not more than three minutes in length, with an introduction, one or two points, and a conclusion. Your teen should be allowed no more than one minute to collect his thoughts and begin speaking.

2. **Topics.** Think of about 50 topics in advance and write them on slips of paper. Topics might include: "My most embarrassing moment," "Something exciting," "Mosquitoes," "My brother (or sister)," "What I would like to be," "My greatest dream," "If I could buy anything…," "The Presidency," "Climbing trees," and "Bubble gum." Let's look at a sample speech on bubble gum. This example may be more complex than your teen will attempt at first, but given practice, he'll improve.

Our topic today is bubble gum. When I think of bubble gum, I remember one horrible experience of chewing bubble gum in school where it was expressly forbidden. After about half an hour, my jaws started to hurt, so I tried to dispose of the gum discreetly. I took it out of my mouth and just then, the teacher got up from her desk! In my haste to cover my misdeed, I dropped the gum. And wouldn't you know it, I dropped it right in the aisle. I learned my lesson that day—actually for about 30 minutes after school that day. Of course, with all of the problems in our schools today, I bet a lot of teachers would wish for the kind of problem I caused that day! In response to that I say, "Get rid of the guns and knives and bring back bubble gum!"

FUTURE ADVENTURE

After some practice, move on to "extemporaneous" speeches, in which the speaker has 30 minutes to prepare a speech and memorize it. These speeches should be on important issues of the day. With manila folders, devise a topical filing system to organize newspaper articles and editorials to use as resources for this kind of speech.

TIMELY TIP

The secret to impromptu speaking is using the 60 seconds of preparation time to think of a couple of main points, and if there is time left, one quick, memorable example. Don't try to think about what words to use. As your teen becomes more proficient, make topics increasingly complex. Your teen should be able to move on to more difficult topics after about 20 speeches.

MAKE IT MEMORABLE!

Try impromptu speaking yourself! This is a family exercise, so do not ask your teen to do what *you* are unwilling to do. Take turns drawing topics and giving speeches!

ORGANIZING A SPEECH

Commonplaces and impromptu speeches are the building blocks of effective speaking. However, most speeches are more complex, and must be planned more carefully to have a full effect on the audience. This activity takes you through the steps necessary to devise a speech topic and gives your teen the opportunity to practice various elements of a speech.

How-To

1. WHO IS IT I AM TRYING TO REACH?

A. What is the audience like? Are they business people? Stay-at-home moms? War veterans? Church members? As you reflect on the composition of the audience, perhaps it would be helpful to narrow down their various characteristics to one defining characteristic. Ask yourself, "What one thing, more than anything else, do the members of this audience have in common?"

- Think of possible audiences to whom your teenager might speak, and ask him to write down as many things as he can about the audience. Characteristics to consider include age, gender, race, national origin, economic status, spiritual maturity, and level of education.

B. Why is this audience meeting? What are the audience members' expectations? If you are giving a speech on "How to become involved in the community," you might "spin" your topic for different audiences. For example, if your audience is a Sunday school class, tie community involvement into the audience's sense of their spiritual responsibilities to those around them. If the audience is an Optimist Club, give its already active members ideas on how to persuade *others* to become involved. With a group of high school students, focus on convincing them that high school students can make a difference.

- Make a list of possible speech topics, hypothesizing several possible audiences for each topic. Give the list to your teenager and have him brainstorm ideas about reaching them.

C. **What are the needs of the audience?** Most audiences will unconsciously ask, "What can you do for me?" In other words, audiences may not listen simply because you have something to say. They will listen when they are convinced that they can benefit from the information you give. Your persuasive appeal carries considerably more weight if you understand what makes the audience tick.

- Ask your teenager to reflect on what *motivates* people. What are people really concerned about? Some possible motivations include *service* (doing the will of God or helping others), *status* (good standing in the eyes of others), *security* (self-preservation, financial well-being), *freedom from restraint* (freedom to do as they wish, such as to make beneficial economic and social choices), *attractiveness* (how they appear to others), and *sense of adventure* (how their life can be more exciting and rewarding).

2. WHAT WOULD I LIKE THE AUDIENCE TO DO OR BELIEVE?

There are many different organizational formats for speeches. For the purposes of this chapter, we will focus on speeches to *inform* and speeches to *persuade*.

A central element of these two basic formats is explaining clearly what you want the audience to do or believe. For some reason, audiences tend to miss the main point unless it is clearly and repeatedly stated. One study demonstrated that 70% of audience members, at the end of an average speech, could not describe the main point the speaker was trying to convey! Here are two ideas which combat that tendency:

A. **What do you wish to say?** What is the purpose of the speech? Write down as many ideas as you can, even if it takes several pages. From that list, highlight one point which seems to stick out, and no more than three points which logically explain that one point. Leave everything else for future speeches.

- Once your teen has written down his ideas, ask him to do two things:

  Complete the statement, "This speech is about _____." Use one to four words only.

  Write a topic sentence, such as, "The purpose of this speech is to _____ by _____." As professional speaker Ken Davis warns, "If you can't write the objective of your speech in a single sentence, then either you're trying to say too much or you don't know what you're talking about."

B. **Why is this important?** First, why do you wish to give this speech? Second, why is this topic important to the *audience?*

- Ask your teen to write down as many ideas as he can, based on a topic he chooses or the topics used above. This will help him clarify his thoughts, become convinced of the importance of the topic, and develop enthusiasm about it.

3. HOW CAN I MAKE SURE MY MESSAGE REACHES THE AUDIENCE?

A. How do I get the audience's attention? A speaker can win or lose the audience's attention within the first minute, so the speaker's first words should be carefully planned through an "attention device." Here are a few effective devices:

- **Rhetorical Question.** A rhetorical question is one which gets the audience thinking about your topic. It usually is not a question they can answer immediately, nor should it be. For instance, if you are giving a speech on behalf of a candidate for Congress, you might ask, "Did you realize that today you have the opportunity to make a simple decision which will change Congress forever?" Some popular rhetorical questions include "Did you know _____," "Have you ever _____," "What would happen if _____," or "Do you suppose...?"

- **Storytelling.** Dramatic stories which relate to the topic are highly effective in winning and maintaining the audience's attention. *Personal stories* are often the most effective, because they relate the speaker and his topic and emotionally involve the audience at the same time. Audiences like stories which communicate "shared values." That is, they want to hear about people who have dealt with the same kinds of issues they face. Stories should be short and to the point, contain plot and dialogue, and *clearly relate to the speech topic*.

- **Shocking Statement.** A shocking statement is simply a dramatic statement which focuses the attention of the audience. I once heard a speaker talk about getting the most out of life. He began his speech by boldly and loudly proclaiming, "There is one statistic of which all intellectuals, scientists and social scientists alike are absolutely certain: One out of every one person...*dies*." His shocking statement was funny and somewhat unexpected, thus it was highly effective in winning the audience and drawing them into his subject. When using this technique, remember to take into consideration the sensibilities of the audience. The point of a shocking statement is to get the audience's attention, not disgust them!

- **Dramatic Interpretation.** In my father's college speech course, one student inconspicuously began a speech by saying "Today, we will discuss the issue of self-defense. Why? Because you never know when..." Just then, the classroom door flew open, and in charged a rough-looking individual, shouting at the speaker: "There you are, you little twerp!" The speaker deftly blocked the attack, twisted the attacker around, knocked him to the floor, and sternly admonished, "Now get out of here, and don't come back!" As the attacker scrambled out of the room, the speaker turned to the audience said, "As I was saying, you never know when you will need to defend yourself!" He then demonstrated several simple self-defense maneuvers to his newly invigorated audience!

B. **How do I relate the topic to the audience?** To move the audience to do or believe what you are suggesting, you must point out the inconsistency between what audience members know they ought to be, and what they actually are. If you can show audience members that their actions are not consistent with their behavior, they are likely to stick around to hear how to become consistent again.

C. How do I organize the speech for maximum impact?
The way I listen to speeches changed forever with a sixteen-word piece of advice I heard when I was thirteen years old: *"Tell 'em what you're gonna tell 'em, then tell 'em, then tell 'em what you told 'em."* Effective speakers heed this advice by outlining the topic in the introduction, highlighting the main points in the body of the speech, and then reviewing the main points in the conclusion.

- How does one organize the individual *points* in a speech for maximum impact? One highly effective technique is the S. T. E. P. system taught by Dr. Lee Polk of Baylor University, one of the nation's foremost speech consultants. Here are the elements of the system, along with sample ideas for each point:

In order to describe the S. T. E. P. system, I have tied it into a sample speech on "Remembering Names."

S = STATE

Topic sentence
"The first way to improve your ability to remember people's names is called 'association.'"

T=TRANSLATE

Definition
"To 'associate' something means tying it to something vivid and memorable."

Explanation
"As a memory technique, you would associate the name you want to remember with something that rhymes with it or something about that name that makes it stand out."

Analogy

"Associating the name you want to remember with something memorable is like attaching a permanent name tag to that person."

E=Exemplify

Example

"For example, let's say you meet someone named Fred Eaton. You notice that he is very skinny. You can remember 'Fred' by 'afraid' and 'Eaton,' with 'eating.' So whenever you see ol' skinny Fred Eaton you will remember his name by thinking that he is 'afraid of eating,' that's why he's so skinny."

Personal Experience

"I once met a woman named Mary Friedlander. I discovered that she and her husband had recently moved to the country to begin farming. When I met her, she was wearing jeans and cowboy boots. I remembered her last name by thinking of being 'free in the land,' and her first name by thinking of her being 'merry' living in the country, thus remembering that Mary Friedlander was 'merry' being 'free in the land.'"

P= Prove

Statistic

"I have discovered that I can remember 50% more names, and retain them for about twice as long using this method than just sheer memory power."

Testimony

"Association really works. As Harry Lorayne and Jerry Lucas say in their book entitled The Memory Book, 'You can remember any new piece of information if it is associated to something you already know or remember.'"

Here's how to use the S. T. E. P. system with great effectiveness whether you are giving a speech, writing a paper or merely answering a question: devise an introduction, proceed through the S. T. E. P. system for each main point, and then devise a conclusion. With practice, someone who methodically applies the S. T. E. P. system will be much more organized, and thus sound intelligent. His ideas will be more acceptable to the audience. In addition, habitually organizing one's thoughts in this manner makes it much easier to "think on one's feet."

INFORMATIVE SPEECH

PROJECT SKETCH

The first of the two basic speech formats is the speech to inform. This speech will put your teen's powers of observation to work, allowing him to entertain an audience by imparting new information. In one sense, this kind of speech raises the self-confidence of a teenager because he is speaking on the one topic about which he knows more than anyone else in the audience (with the possible exception of the parent who coached him!).

The topics for such a speech are many and varied; among the fascinating topics I have heard are: how a paper mill works, why some people are left-handed, the history of the railroad in the community, what happens when you sneeze, the truth about brown recluse spiders, and how to improve your golf swing.

HOW-TO

Once your teen has brainstormed and organized the material according to the main point and the needs of the audience, this outline may be used to mold the content into an informative speech format.

I. Introduction (A story or shocking statement).

II. Statement of purpose ("The purpose of this speech is to _____ by _____ .")

III. Background. Give the relevant facts to understanding the subject. Assume the audience knows very little, and provide them with what they need to know to understand the topic.

IV. Initial summary ("In order to more fully explore _____, I am going to take you through _____ steps.")

V. Main Points. Usually an audience can remember three to four main points. *Organize each main point using the S. T. E. P. system*, described in the project on "Organizing a Speech."

        State
        Translate
            Definition
            Explanation
            Analogy
        Exemplify
            Example
            Personal Experience
        Prove
            Statistic
            Testimony

VI. Focus. Tell the audience what you want them to understand and remember from the presentation.

VII. Conclusion ("In conclusion, _____.")

FUTURE ADVENTURE

Combine the informative speech with a demonstration speech. Your teen can fuse the two forms together to create a presentation in which to teach the audience a practical skill such as first aid, lifesaving, or map and compass reading.

MAKE IT MEMORABLE!

Teach your teen to teach. Show him how to use the informative speech format to explain how to do a particular job. Even if the presentation is not as detailed, and even if your teen is training only one person, it is still excellent experience in a practical life skill.

NOTES

PERSUASIVE SPEECH

PROJECT SKETCH

The second of the two basic speech formats is the speech to persuade. The goal of such a speech is to persuade the audience to either 1) change their beliefs, attitudes or values, or 2) act on what you are telling them. Writing and practicing persuasive speeches is the most practical, helpful way to understand the nature of persuasion and how to become a more persuasive person.

HOW-TO

Review the "Organizing a Speech" project and ask your teen to organize the speech material into a persuasive format. Here is an outline of the most rudimentary persuasive speech, a speech to persuade the audience that a certain problem exists:

I. Introduction (a story or example).

II. Statement of need or problem ("My point today is that we face a serious problem, 'X.'").

III. Explanation of need or problem.

A. Undesirable effects ("Some of the consequences of 'X' problem are 'A,' 'B,' and 'C.'").

B. Extensiveness ("How far ranging is 'X' problem? According to _____, an expert on the subject, it is _____ .").

C. Personal experience ("Perhaps my personal experience with 'X' problem will shed some light on it...").

IV. Conclusion ("As we close...").

FUTURE ADVENTURE

When your teen is ready, he can move on to a more complex persuasive speech, one designed to persuade the audience to take action:

I. Introduction (a story or example).

II. Review of the problem/need ("You may be quite familiar with 'X' problem. But just to review...").

III. Statement of Solution/Plan ("I would like to present a plan that will remedy problem 'X.'").

   A. Explanation of the plan ("Here is how the plan operates...").

   B. An example of what would be different with this plan in effect ("How would this plan look in action? Let me give an example...").

   C. Proof that the plan will work ("A plan very similar to this one was tried in _____. The results demonstrated conclusively that the plan can do what it promises to do. Here are some of the benefits of that plan...").

IV Advantages of the plan ("Just so we're all clear, here are the specific advantages of the plan...").

V. Call to specific action ("Based on what I have presented, there is a specific action you can take...").

TIMELY TIP

First, these formats are not intended to *confine* the speaker but to *guide* him in including the essential elements.

Within each main point refer back to the "S. T. E. P. system" proposed in the chapter on organizing a speech. Second, allow time for preparation. This kind of speech usually takes a couple of days to assemble. Assist your teen in finding a dramatic story and some quotes which can serve as evidence. Gradually, he should be able to do this on his own.

MAKE IT MEMORABLE!

Find audiences. Your teen can give his completed speech to guests you have in your home, your co-workers, the family, and if possible the church. He must have the opportunity to give his speech as many times as possible. Practice is the key to speech success!

NOTES

BIOGRAPHICAL SPEECH PROJECT

ONE
WAY
➡

PROJECT SKETCH

A biographical speech is an informative or persuasive speech which highlights the character qualities of a hero from Christian history. The purpose of the biographical speech is to provide an exciting speech project with the side benefits of familiarizing your teen with the deep and wonderful heritage he enjoys as a Christian. It will help him recognize the admirable qualities of great men and women of the faith, using them as role models for his own life of leadership.

HOW-TO

1. **Select a hero.** Use your best judgement in deciding which hero of the faith would be most appropriate. It is probably best to give your teen lots of choices and allow him to select one who sounds interesting. The speech should focus on the biblical character qualities held by that person. Consider choosing a hero who lived *after* Bible times and that you personally do not know. One purpose of this project is to learn about the influence of Christians on culture through the ages.

Here are just a few Christians who have been widely noted and are therefore easier to research: Abigail Adams, John Quincy Adams, Gladys Aylward, Johann Sebastian Bach, William Blackstone, Deitrich Bonhoeffer, William Booth, John Calvin, Amy Carmichael, George Washington Carver, Catherine of Vienna, Fanny Crosby, Elizabeth Fry, George Frederick Handel, C. S. Lewis, Martin Luther, Henrietta Mears, D. L. Moody, Mother Teresa, Florence Nightingale, Mary Slessor, Charles Spurgeon, Hudson Taylor, Corrie

Ten Boom, Harriet Tubman, Isaac Watts, Noah Webster, Susanna Wesley (John's mother) and William Wilberforce.

2. Create a clear outline.

I. Introduction

II. Background of the hero's life (what he or she did while young in preparation for influencing others, family influences, etc.)

III. The outstanding character quality the person possessed

A. Definition of the quality and scripture verse about it

B. Example of how the person displayed that quality

C. How that quality affected the person's life

IV. A memorable quote from that person

V. Conclusion

FUTURE ADVENTURE

1. **A campaign speech.** Your teen can pretend that the hero he has chosen is running for political office today. What kind of things could that person contribute based on their actions during their lifetime?

2. **A "This is Your Life" play.** Dress up as the character, or use a "reader's theater" format with a single light, stool, and dramatic script. Tell the story as if you are really that person. Several videos of this nature are available, and you can often find people portraying

historical characters in this way at historical gatherings and events. Done well, this type of activity is *extremely* popular and stands to win your teenager many speaking engagements!

TIMELY TIP

How do you find heroes? Consult books such as *Foxe's Book of Martyrs*, *The Light and the Glory* by Peter Marshall, Jr. and David Manuel, *Men and Women We Call Heroes* by Ann Spangler, and *Lives of Famous Christians* by Tony Castle. There are also several series of biographies for children published by Bethany House Publishers and Mott Media. Also, examine the biographical history magazine *Christian History Today*.

MAKE IT MEMORABLE!

Prepare a Sunday school lesson. Your teen can prepare a lesson about the character qualities of his hero in order to help others grow in character.

NOTES

VIDEO OR RADIO PLAYS

Project Sketch

Media is so advanced today that a course in communication would not be complete without at least a short introduction to communication technology. You may find that your teen is interested in knowing more about radio or television, or you may conduct the project simply to give him a greater awareness of how it works. One way to create awareness is to actually write a script and conduct a video or radio play. Your teen will gain an understanding of persuasion, vocal enthusiasm, mood, sequence, and drama.

How-To

1. **Radio play.** A radio play is simply a story read out loud. The only equipment required is a tape recorder. Encourage your teen to plan the play so it can be recorded all at one time, like an old-fashioned "live" radio broadcast, including sound effects. Here are the necessary steps:

   A. **Conceive a story line, complete with a plot, action, suspense, and resolution.**

   B. **Write the story in the form of a play with each character's lines and directions.**

   C. **Choose actors or work on the voices of the various characters.**

   D. **Select sound effects and work on timing.**

   E. Select music.

2. **Video play.** Create a "television program" using a video camera. The steps mentioned above are the same, but additional work is required. Experiment with the camera to get a feel for lighting, zoom, etc. The "action" should be planned out on a story board, which is a page of squares representing television screens in which each scene is "blocked." Plan out as much as possible on paper first. Here are some things to consider: How is the lighting? Might I choose a better camera angle to get more detail or make the action more suspenseful? Are my actors using facial expressions that are pronounced enough to be seen on camera? Am I holding the camera steady and not zooming in and out too much?

FUTURE ADVENTURES

1. **Mock news broadcast.** Use the material from your current events studies to put together a news program. Video or audio tape it and review. To see how this is done in the real world, tour a local television or radio station and obtain permission to watch quietly during a news broadcast.

2. **Create a video advertisement or documentary.** Use the video camera to assemble a mock promotional video or documentary of an interesting historical site or a business.

TIMELY TIP

Examine a lot of samples. Your library probably owns a collection of video documentaries and audio tapes of old radio plays. Contact Moody Broadcasting in Chicago, Illinois, about their radio plays of great figures in Christian history. Also, children's radio plays are available from Children's Bible Hour in Grand Rapids, Michigan. Get as many tapes as you can to collect ideas. Using videotape equipment proficiently requires practice. Give your teen opportunities to practice by creatively videotaping events such as family reunions, picnics, and vacations. He can even think of a running dialogue to give while filming.

MAKE IT MEMORABLE!

Allow your teen to create a video documentary of his hero of history from the biographical speech project. Using pictures and simulated scenes from their life, compose a five minute presentation.

NOTES

SLIDE SHOW

PROJECT SKETCH

A slide show is a simpler, more controlled version of the radio and video play project. It is especially good for teens who are terrified of being in front of an audience. The goal of the project is to create a slide presentation of an interesting subject with "live" narration. The focus is on both visual and oral communication, and since the audience's attention is on the screen, a shy teenager can practice communication skills without the pressure of being "up front."

HOW-TO

1. **Select a subject.** The topic may be the youth group missions trip, a historical narrative of a famous person who grew up in your town, a study of a historical monument or event, or even a made-up story.

2. **Take pictures.** Be sure to purchase lots of slide film. Plan for approximately 20 slides for each minute of presentation.

3. **Write a speech to go along with the show.** Plan out what to say just as with a speech. Devise an interesting introduction, several main points, and supporting evidence (stories, examples and quotes).

FUTURE ADVENTURES

1. **Record the speech.** Write out a word-for-word script and read it on to the tape, along with music and other sound effects. Include interviews and color commentary.

2. Use slides as another means of conducting a demonstration speech or biographical speech.

TIMELY TIPS

1. **Take a lot of pictures!** Your teen should take two or three shots of everything he wants in the presentation, to make sure that at least one turns out. Try different angles, and make sure that the subject of the slide is immediately obvious.

2. **Watch the time!** Slide shows always seem to be too *short* to express the presenter's level of interest, but too *long* for the audience's level of interest. Make the presentation concise; it is always better to leave them wanting than to have them wanting to leave.

MAKE IT MEMORABLE!

Use this project as a spring board. A slide show is an excellent communication activity for a shy child, but it should not be the only project he does. Start with this, move on to a puppet show, and eventually a Sunday school lesson for younger children. Your goal as a parent is to take your teen as far as you can in the development of his communication skills, so continue to love, instruct, praise, encourage and challenge him!

ADVERTISING CAMPAIGN

PROJECT SKETCH

One fun and motivating project which will help your teen understand elements of persuasion is to assemble an advertising campaign. Many teens have actually decided to create and market a real product! Even a mock campaign, however, will give your teen an awareness of what advertising is and does, how advertising is persuasive, and how to be a better consumer.

HOW-TO

Create a mock advertising scenario, ask your teen to create one, or have him create a campaign for something he actually wants to sell. Here are five steps to developing an advertising campaign:

1. **Outline a means of presenting the product.** Decide on a name and a campaign theme.

2. **Analyze the market, and write a short report.** This should include *who* the product will be sold to, *what* they are like, and *how much* they might be willing to spend. Interview some people in the target group. Would they buy a product like this and how much would they pay for it? Even if the product is not a real one, your teen should nevertheless ask people to choose from several possible prices.

3. **Choose media.** This is an information gathering stage. Every company that sells advertising prints a "media kit" which explains how many people you could reach if you buy their advertising space and what it costs. Collect media kits from radio stations,

television stations, newspapers, billboard companies, bus and taxi companies, printers, mailing companies and "premium" companies (those who sell logo key chains, pens, coffee mugs, etc.). Examine the materials, deciding how to reach the most people. Establish a budget that includes several different kinds of advertising.

4. **Write the campaign.** Prepare "mock up" advertisements:

A. **Magazine page.** Include copy and artwork.

B. **Script and story board for a 30-second television commercial.** Draw out the action with stick figures—one scene per box, writing the script underneath the appropriate square.

C. **Script for a 15- or 30-second radio commercial.** Record it onto tape with an enthusiastic voice, using music or sound effects as needed.

D. **Poster.** Design a "poster," to be used on a billboard, bus, or store display.

5. **Prepare a presentation.** As the "expert," prepare a presentation "selling" the advertising strategy, justify it and explain the benefits.

FUTURE ADVENTURE

Offer to plan a real-world campaign for your church to promote the Sunday school program or Vacation Bible School. Volunteer for a political campaign and observe how they use their resources to influence as many people as possible.

TIMELY TIPS

Review the exercise on "Interviewing" in this section to assist your teen in compiling a market survey.

MAKE IT MEMORABLE!

Analyze "real-world" advertisements. Ask questions such as, "What makes it effective?" "What evidence supports their claim?", "How do we know the evidence is reliable?", "Is the proof they give the most convincing evidence they had?", "What appeals does the advertisement use?", "What audience are they targeting?" and "What might they have done *more* effectively?"

More about Jeff Myers' company:

Dr. Jeff Myers is President of the Myers Institute for Communication and Leadership. Through the Myers Institute, Dr. Myers offers seminars, video coaching systems, books and newsletters which help people unleash their gifts, find greater meaning and satifaction in life, and expend their influence. To find out about these resources, and to sign-up for Dr.Myers' free weekly e-mail coaching tips newsletter, visit the Myers Institute website www.inspiredleadership. com or call toll free 1-888-792-4445.

Here are three resources published by the Myers Institute which will help you and your family gain the skills you need to succeed. These may be ordered with a MasterCard or Visa by calling toll free 1-888-792-4445 or by visiting the website www.inspiredleadership.com.

Secrets of Great Communicators: Simple, Powerful Strategies for Reaching the Heart of Your Audience. The six-step video coaching system makes speaking to a crowd as simple and natural as singing in the shower! Many people think that public speaking is mysterious gift, but Dr.Myers demonstrates how anyone can master this vital skill and dramatically expand their confidence, poise and image. The video coaching lessons reveal the secrets of great communicators, and the 160 page study guide leads you step by step through overcoming your fear, organizing a presentation, tapping into power persuasion, and delivering your message to the heart of the audience.

Secrets of the World-Changers: How to Achieve Lasting Influence as a Leader. Looking for more joy, meaning, satisfaction and influence in life? This fast-paced video coaching system helps you achieve a strategic vision, break through the "noise" of culture to understand your unique mission in life, stay motivated through the tough times, and set goals that really work. Secrets of the World-Changers comes complete with an easy-to-use 75 page reproducible study guide. This coaching system has been used by more than 1,500 schools, athletic teams, study groups and homeschool co-ops to instill leadership skills in youth and adults alike.

Of Knights and Fair Maidens: A Radical New Way to Develop Old-Fashioned Relationships. Before their marriage, both Jeff and Danielle had been seaching for alternatives to the dating game. This book tells the funny, heart-winning story of how they got to know each other through old-fashioned courtship principles. Jeff and Danielle reveal the three keys to integrity in relationships to demonstrate how following God's Principles leads to joy, trust and romance.